SAVE ME!

The

Financially Wi$e

Girl's Quick Guide to Saving

Kathy Ran

Copyright © 2015 Kathy Ran

All rights reserved.

ISBN: 150308261X
ISBN-13: 978-1503082618

Dedication

For my children, Ingrid and Ian, who inspire me every day to be a better person and to strive for a better future.

Kathy Ran

Save Me! The Financially Wise Girl's Quick Guide to Saving

Preface

Welcome to the Financially Wise series of financial books for women who want to take control of their finances.

There are five books in this beginners series to help you become financially wise and financially free:

1. Save Me! The Financially Wi$e Girl's Quick Guide to Saving
2. Before You Buy That! The Financially Wi$e Girl's Quick Guide to Budgeting
3. Oops, Overdrawn! The Financially Wi$e Girl's Quick Guide to Eliminating Debt
4. Turn Those Taps On! The Financially Wi$e Girl's Quick Guide to Creating Multiple Streams of Income
5. Finally Free! The Financially Wi$e Girl's Quick Guide to Calculating Retirement Income.

If there is one (or more) specific area on which you'd like to improve your knowledge and take action, the books are written so they can be read in isolation. However, if you'd like to take control of most or all facets of your financial life, you can read the entire series. The list above is in the recommended reading order.

You decide what level you are at and what information you require to achieve your desired outcome for your financial goals. Don't leave it to someone else, or assume that anyone else has your best financial interests at heart. Nobody cares about your financial wellbeing as much as you do.

I'd like to introduce myself and share with you how this series of books came about. My name is Kathy Ran and I once had the same beliefs, mindset and complete lack of knowledge about money that seems so prevalent now. However, the shock of being left with a six-figure debt after a marriage breakdown in the mid-2000s made me realise that I needed to change my life and become financially wiser.

I started to actively search out financial information, read books and attend seminars. I learned a lot, changed my mindset about money, started applying what I'd learned and, best of all, I paid off my debts. Since then I have dedicated a huge part of my life and invested time and money on educating myself and learning all I could about finance and investing. I'd like to now share some of what I've learned with you and help you on your journey to increasing your financial knowledge.

This knowledge has helped many other people overcome their financial problems, achieve their goals and ambitions and make the journey to financial independence and freedom.

If you follow the very simple steps outlined in this book, combined with the knowledge of why you need to do this, you will be well on your way to financial independence and freedom and ahead of so many other people.

So congratulations on taking steps to educate yourself financially. Being financially literate not only gives you more options, it also allows you to more fully understand various investments and make better decisions regarding your future.

My hope is that one day schools across the world teach these basic and fundamental financial principles from early childhood. Until then I will continue to educate and involve you in reading and educating yourself through my series of Financially Wise books.

Kathy Ran

Disclaimer

This information is of a general nature only and is provided "as is". The author, publishers and marketers of this information do not know your individual circumstances and are therefore unable to provide specific financial advice and disclaim any loss or liability, either directly or indirectly as a consequence of applying the information presented herein, or in regard to the use and application of said information. No guarantee is given, either expressed or implied, in regard to the merchantability, accuracy, or acceptability of the information. It is strongly recommended that the reader do their own research and investigation before entering into any financial arrangement and seek professional advice where applicable.

Table of Contents

1 Introduction 1
    The Basics 3
2 Why Should You Save Money? 9
3 Demographics: a Quick Lesson 13
4 What is Your Vision – Your Why? 22
5 Finding Your Hidden Cash 28
6 Your Team 37
7 Putting a Savings Plan into Action 43
8 Money Saving Areas 52
9 Ten Months Later 86
10 End Note 88
Resources 89
The other Financially Wise Books in this beginners series 91
About the Author 95

Acknowledgments

I'd like to thank all those people who helped me to make this book what it is.

To all my long suffering family and friends, who were pressed into reading the manuscript in its various forms – Alysia, Ellen, Daniela, Ingrid and Lorelle, thank you from the bottom of my heart for your editing, assessing, proofreading, suggested changes and unbelievably useful feedback. To my editor Sally, thanks for all your corrections, suggestions and patience. Also Donna, Helen, Mary, Marie, Patricia and everyone else who provided me with invaluable advice. Thanks to Jan for the photography and Narelle for the cover design.

Thank you everyone who believed in me and encouraged me to follow my dream of bringing these books to fruition.

And to the readers of this book, thank you for sharing your valuable time and money to invest in yourself. I hope you gain some wisdom and clarity.

1 INTRODUCTION

"Money is a good servant but a bad master"
French Proverb

"What's the matter, you look deep in thought? Penny for them?" Sage Hibou enquired as she walked past her friend, Daria, who was sitting on the front steps of her apartment block. Daria was absently tapping a pen against an open notebook.

"I'm trying to think of ways I can make some money. I really need to upgrade my old car now that I'm working on the other side of town and taking those night classes at college. But I'm just not sure I can afford it," Daria said ruefully, gazing at her old, beaten-up car, parked outside the apartment building.

Sage looked thoughtfully at the car in question. It had certainly seen better days and was becoming quite unreliable, despite the best efforts of the local mechanic, who was losing the battle to keep the car running. Because of its age, parts were becoming more difficult to source and some things couldn't be repaired any more.

She peered down at Daria's notebook. It was blank.

"Why can't you afford to buy another car?" she asked Daria. "How much have you got in savings?"

Daria looked uncomprehendingly at her friend. "Savings?" she asked. "I don't have any savings. I spend everything as soon as I make it, and then use my credit cards to make up the difference."

Sage shook her head in disbelief. "You don't save any of your income? Nothing at all?" she asked incredulously. "What do you do if you have an emergency?"

Daria shrugged. "I fight that fire when I cross that bridge," she said mixing her metaphors.

Her face brightened as she looked at Sage. "Hey," she began, "you're good with money, maybe you can help me. Teach me everything you know. We weren't taught any money skills at school, and I'm not learning anything about good money management at college."

Sage nodded, considering. "I agree that financial knowledge is sadly lacking in all our schools and universities – nobody is taught how money works. It's why so many people get into trouble with money. And because it's not taught at any level, this lack of knowledge is passed down from one generation to the next."

She paused for a moment, before coming to a decision. "Yes," she said, "I'll teach you what I know about money and finance. It's important for you right now because you really need to replace your car, but it will be more important for you in the future as you start to earn more money, look at buying a place to live, get married, have children and plan for your old age."

She smiled. "You'll be my student in all things financial. I'll be a member of team Daria. My name in French actually means wise owl, so I will become your Wise Owl mentor."

Daria laughed and then said thoughtfully, nodding, "Wise Owl? Yes, I like it. It certainly has a ring to it and it suits you."

She chuckled. "My name means wealthy or affluent in Greek. I'm not yet, but I hope I'll grow into it once you've taught me the basics. Let's start right now."

"OK," said Wise Owl. "I'll go over some basics first and then we can work our way towards setting up a savings plan. The basics are important to understand so you know why you need to have financial knowledge."

Daria got her pen and notebook ready and sat back in expectation.

The Basics

[You can skip this section if you have already read this in one of the other books, although it is recommended that you reread these sections in each book. The stories may be different to fit in with the topic.]

Wise Owl began, "Knowledge of money and how it works is a fundamental requirement. However, as I mentioned earlier, the subject of finance, investing and good money management is not generally taught at school, nor is it considered important enough to become part of an accepted curriculum. Unless your parents are wealthy or knowledgeable, you don't learn it from them either. Therefore this lack of knowledge is perpetuated throughout generations and the same thoughts, beliefs and mistakes around money continue to be made."

Daria shook her head. Her parents did not fall into either the wealthy or financially knowledgeable category.

Wise Owl continued, "Women in particular are almost universally disadvantaged financially. Not only do they consistently earn less than men, ensuring that they have less to save and invest to begin with, they also generally live longer. They are usually the primary children's caregiver, which removes them from the workforce and further limits their earning capacity. Women are also usually worse off after a divorce, particularly if there are children involved.

"During the last century we were practically brainwashed into studying hard at school and university to achieve good grades. Why? So we could get a good job that paid well and had plenty of benefits. And once again why did we need this? To service the perpetual debt we must all have to buy more 'stuff'. Our mindsets are consumer driven rather than investor driven.

"We've been told not to worry about the future because firstly our employer will look after us. And then later when we retire, the government will take over that responsibility. But for those who come of age in the new millennium, this paradigm no longer applies. In the 21st century we can no longer afford to keep this mindset. Furthermore, our education system has simply not kept up with the changing world. Schools around the world are still teaching students to be employees rather than entrepreneurs and business owners. But many jobs available today simply won't be here ten years from now and our schools teach things that are increasingly irrelevant and are preparing students to enter a world which has changed and doesn't really exist anymore."

Daria nodded and thought of some of the things she had been required to learn at school – things that had completely confused her, didn't interest her and which would have no bearing or use in her life. "What a waste of time that was," she murmured. "I could have been learning something useful, like how to manage my money, rather than let someone else do that."

$$\sqrt[3]{4}$$

Wise Owl agreed. "We need to take back control of our finances and not entrust our future wealth to someone else. We need to learn all the basic financial skills required to operate successfully in the 21st Century and beyond.

"Finance and money impacts on every facet of our life, whether we like it or not, and even whether we are aware of it or not.

"And it's true that there are things that money can't buy, like love or happiness. But try and pay an electricity or phone bill or buy some groceries or a car or house or education tuition using anything other than money.

"Most of us are so busy making sure everyone else gets paid, that we forget to pay ourselves first, or even at all. But this is the wrong way around and the opposite of what we should do.

"The time has come to change our mindset from consumer to investor and take control of our own finances."

"I'd like to share a story with you." Wise Owl said to Daria. "It may help to explain why you need to become financially educated and savvy..."

Barbara married her high school sweetheart at 19 and fell pregnant within the first year of marriage, after working only six months at the local kindergarten. Her husband started work at the local hardware store and, after the birth of their first child, it was agreed that he should be the breadwinner while she stayed at home and looked after the children. He did so well in the hardware business, he ended up buying his own store and several more in the surrounding areas. Barbara was given an allowance for shopping and money to spend on herself while her husband took care of all the "financial stuff", such as paying all the bills, looking after insurances, motor vehicle expenses and other so called "men's business." They lived well and never seemed to be short of money. She managed to raise four children and began to look forward to the enjoyment of travelling the world with her husband once he retired from his business in a few years' time.

So it was an enormous shock when he died unexpectedly in a car accident. She did not even have time to recover from the grief of losing not just her husband, but all her future retirement plans, when their accountant and lawyer told her the bad news. Her husband was deeply in debt with his businesses, borrowing from shop to shop to cover business expenses and he had not only re-mortgaged their home, he had taken out a second mortgage as well. Worse still, he had let a number of insurances, including his life insurance, lapse to save money, intending to take out policies again once things picked up.

For Barbara, it was a very steep financial learning curve. She had never even paid as much as a utility bill on their home let alone understood the day-to-day running of a business. Fortunately, with the help of the accountant and lawyer, she was able to sell the businesses to pay off the various creditors, and sell her home to cover the mortgages. With some prudent advice, careful saving and help from her children, she managed to buy a small apartment for herself to live out her retirement years.

"Think about that for a moment," Wise Owl said. "This example is probably extreme, and reflects a time when women weren't expected to know or even take an interest in anything to do with financial matters. A time when it wasn't the done thing, or polite, to talk about money. But the story highlights how common it is for people to become exposed because they don't have the correct knowledge.

"Barbara was extremely lucky that her story ended as well as it did. For many women, it does not end well at all, with some women having to return to work at 50 or 60 and having to sell the family home and find rental accommodation because there is simply no money.

"There is the other extreme as well, where a widowed woman is left with some assets, which if handled carefully and invested correctly should last through her retirement and remainder of life. However, due to poor decision making and lack of knowledge about managing money and assets wisely, it often doesn't last or is lost."

Daria nodded sombrely. "I could be any of those women."

"Exactly!" Wise Owl agreed.

"It's said that money makes a very good servant, but a poor master. Knowledge is the key. You need to master your finances by becoming financially wise. You need to be educated on financial matters. You can't afford not to know.

"So right now Daria, it's time to think about your finances and for you to take control of them." Wise Owl said.

Wise Owl stopped to check her watch. "I think that's enough to begin with, to encourage you to start thinking differently about your money. We'll continue with your lessons tomorrow and discuss why saving is a good thing."

Daria nodded and got up from the stairs. "See you then." she said.

FINANCIALLY WISE ACTION PLAN –

Start to think about how you can take active control of your finances.

What areas of your financial life are controlled by someone else?

Who is making these decisions? A financial planner? A banker?

Do you have investments, a mortgage, personal loan or credit card and do you decide the returns, terms and conditions or interest rate?

List some ways you can control your own finances, what you need to know to take back control and by when (timeframe).

Notes:

_____

_____

_____

_____

_____

_____

_____

_____

_____

_____

2 WHY SHOULD YOU SAVE MONEY?

"Only boys who save their pennies make my rainy day."
Madonna, Material Girl

"Right," said Wise Owl when they caught up again the next evening. "Are you ready to begin?"

"Well," began Daria, "I was watching television last night and I noticed there were a lot of advertisements from banks offering loans that seemed easy to get with very low interest rates, and credit cards that had fairly high limits. There were even car companies offering finance on their new cars. It all seems so easy. Why do I even need to save money at all?"

? ? ?

Wise Owl nodded and considered. "That is a good question indeed – I'm glad you asked. Why? Why should you save money when it is so easy to obtain credit cards and bank loans?"

Daria hurriedly added, "I still intend to start saving though, I was just wondering, as nobody seems to save anymore."

Wise Owl said. "Yes, it's a lost art. But saving is a good discipline and one that can help you achieve not just your short-term wants, like a car, TV or holiday, but your long-term financial goals as well. Many people live from pay to pay with no thought of how they might support themselves should something happen to them and they are no longer able to work."

Daria nodded guiltily.

Wise Owl continued. "They have no buffer in place to cushion any emergencies. The sooner you start a savings plan, the more it will become an ingrained habit and a discipline. The savings habit is one of the cornerstones to your financial success.

"Let me share another story with you..."

When Jennie started school in the 1970s, her parents opened a savings account for her, since her school participated in a savings scheme with the local bank. She faithfully made weekly deposits, firstly organised by her mother and then, as she grew older, doing the paperwork herself as she continued to add weekly deposits into her savings.

Even when the school stopped participating in the savings scheme and she moved to high school, she continued to make regular deposits into her account, using savings to purchase things she wanted rather than waiting for birthdays and Christmas.

By the time she left school, started university and had a part-time job, she had saved enough to buy herself a second-hand car. By the time she had graduated with her degree, she had been able to go on a number of overseas holidays, and within five years of working full time, she had saved enough to pay a considerable deposit of over 40% of the purchase price for her first property.

Saving money was an ingrained habit that was a firm part of who she was.

Daria nodded impressed.

Wise Owl continued "Your savings habits will change depending on what your stage of life is. When you are single and working, it can be much easier to save than when you are married and have a family. However, if you make it a priority, it can be achieved."

"We have, on the whole, turned from being savers to spenders, relying far too much on credit and increasingly living beyond our means by spending more than we earn. An alarming number of people are only three pay cycles away from bankruptcy. Statistics indicate that a significant proportion of the population is spending over 100% and as much as 150% of their income. They use credit to finance their lives. Or put another way, they are using tomorrow's income to fund today's consumption."

Daria was quiet for a moment. "I never thought of it in that way. That I was actually using my future income to pay for what I spent today. I assumed that there would always be future income for me and never thought about what might happen if there suddenly wasn't."

She shook her head. "I really wasted all those opportunities to save some of my income, for so long."

Wise Owl then shook her head in turn. "Don't think like that – the past is the past and what's done is done. You can't change your past, but you have full control of your future. You can start right now. It is never too early or too late to start saving.

"It's about living within your means or in other words, spending less than you earn. This is something you can learn." She stood up and stretched. "We'll continue with the lessons tomorrow when we look at demographics and what it means for all of us."

Daria looked surprised. "Demographics? Really? Why is that important and what does it have to do with saving?"

Wise Owl grinned and said, "All in good time. Tomorrow, all will be revealed."

FINANCIALLY WISE ACTION PLAN –

Investigate high interest, low bank fee savings accounts. Find one that meets your specific criteria and open a new account.

Notes:

_____

_____

_____

_____

_____

_____

_____

_____

3 DEMOGRAPHICS: A QUICK LESSON

"On a long enough timeline, the survival rate for everyone drops to zero."
Zerohedge website - www.zerohedge.com

[You can skip this section if you have already read this in one of the other books, although it is recommended that you reread these sections in each book.]

"Okay." said Wise Owl the following day when the lesson began after lunch at Daria's place. "Let's continue with our lessons."

"Yes." said Daria, "Demographics you said yesterday. Why do I need to know about that and what does it have to do with me and saving money?"

"Well," Wise Owl said, "It's another consideration on why you need to save money and why you need to start saving soon."

She paused for a moment, deep in thought.

"Look, it is important you start a savings plan. But before we get into the nuts and bolts of that I'd like to begin with some background information to help with your understanding of the way things currently are and why they can't continue this way in the 21st Century," Wise Owl said.

"Much of the world experienced an unusual phenomenon after the Second World War, known as the Baby Boom period. The generation of Baby Boomers were not like previous generations as they caused an anomaly and unusual occurrence in global demographics.

"Because of the sheer number of Baby Boomers, a statistical irregularity was created in the population demographics of pretty much every developed country after the war, which has had far-reaching effects. This generation saw unprecedented prosperity and growth and, unlike their wartime parents, lived with abundance not lack.

"What this did was create an expectation that this was the norm, that there would always be good times and everyone could have everything now. These times also coincided with an exponential growth of technology, increases in credit availability and advances in medicine, thus prolonging life. But this created problems for the generations that came after them.

"Because the Baby Boom was one of great economic growth and prosperity, governments were able to create a large number of welfare programs. Companies became prosperous because there was a huge demand for goods as Baby Boomers grew up, passed through university education, found jobs, married and had children. Companies and economies grew at tremendous rates, sometimes in double digits, and more people became employed. As the tax base grew, government revenues continued to increase allowing funding for various programs, including a cradle to grave welfare system, which was not possible previously.

Wise Owl paused for a sip of water before continuing. "Asset prices, particularly real estate and stocks, increased."

"That's all good though, isn't it?" asked Daria.

"Oh yes," Wise Owl replied, "but this is a double-edged sword. Because in all but a very few select countries, the generations that came after the Baby Boomers have been smaller. In order to maintain the level of welfare now expected, each succeeding generation must be larger than the previous one. But that hasn't happened.

"Unfortunately, it became the norm for governments to keep promising more and more at each election in order to get elected. But this is only possible if there are sufficient additional workers from the succeeding generation to foot the bill."

Wise Owl paused and said, "I'll draw you a chart which might help you to understand that better." She took Daria's notebook and drew a diagram.

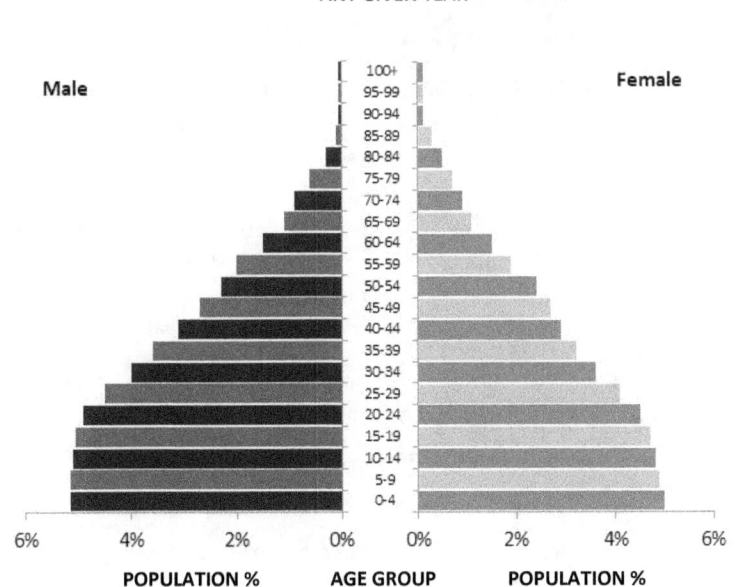

"You can see in this model that there are more young people than older people," Wise Owl said showing it to Daria.

"But in many countries, both developed and developing, this has not occurred. The figures look more like this..." and she drew another diagram and passed the notebook back to Daria.

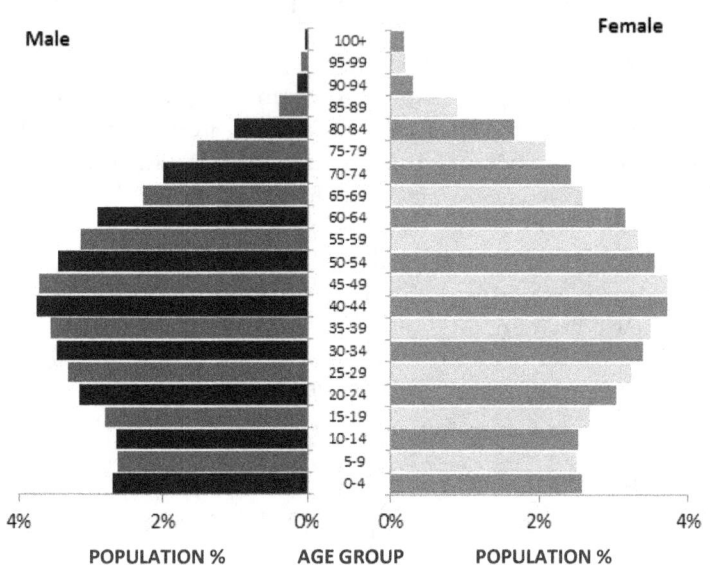

"Less younger people. A smaller subsequent generation," remarked Daria.

"Exactly!" agreed Wise Owl, "And this has created disastrous consequences.

"In order to fully understand these consequences, we need to go back 100 or so years and look at the history of how our welfare state came about."

Daria leaned forward. "Yes, I'd like to know why our politicians seem to be so concerned about all that."

Wise Owl smiled and continued. "The pension system is not new. It has been in existence for quite a few hundred years, but it was usually only available to soldiers or those who defended their country or King or Queen of the day." She paused. "Well, those who survived, of course.

"However, as the feudal system began to vanish, pressure was on to create a more universal pension system. This was firstly achieved by Otto von Bismarck, the German Chancellor from 1881 to 1891, who is generally credited with creating the modern welfare state.

"After he had succeeded in uniting Germany, to win over the conservatives, he proposed certain measures including a universal pension, unemployment insurance, accident insurance and medical care. When von Bismarck proposed a pension, he arbitrarily chose between 65 and 70 as the age that workers could retire and claim a pension from the state."

Daria nodded slowly, perplexed. It all seemed perfectly reasonable to her.

Wise Owl continued, "However, at that time the life expectancy of workers was about 45 years of age, so there was little expectation of many claims to a pension, as few people were expected to live long enough to do so."

"Oh," said Daria startled in realisation. "So there were hardly any retired people claiming pensions at that time? Unlike now."

"No. Not at all like now," Wise Owl replied. "When other countries decided to implement pension systems, for example, Australia and the UK in the early 1900s and the US in the 1930s, 65 for men and 60 for women was also selected as the age that pensions could be claimed as they used the German precedent. However, once again, life expectancies at the time were early to mid-50s, with few making it to their 60s. At best people could expect a few years of pension before passing on.

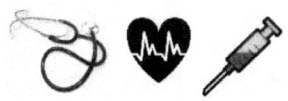

"Then, during the post war years, advances in medicine exploded and people began living longer. Life expectancy has steadily increased in most developed countries to the 70s and 80s. I'll draw it in a chart," she said, taking Daria's notebook again.

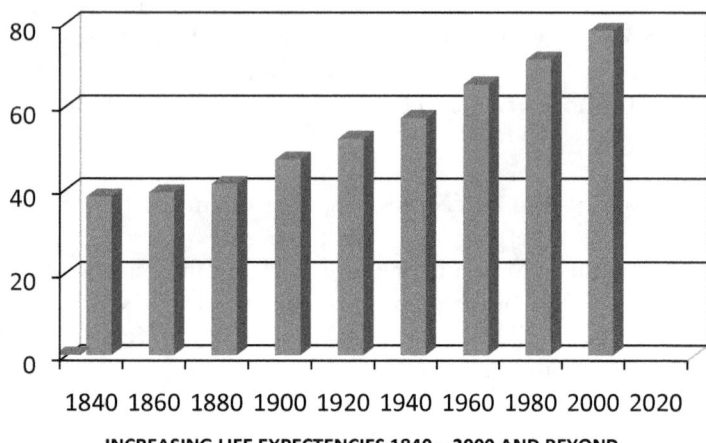

INCREASING LIFE EXPECTENCIES 1840 – 2000 AND BEYOND

Wise Owl passed the notebook back to Daria, who looked carefully at the new diagram and the previous ones.

"Right, I see," she said. "People are living longer and later generations are decreasing."

"The figures vary depending on where you are in the world of course," Wise Owl stated. "But life expectancies are increasing in general and the pension eligibility age is not being adjusted up in line with this. This means that it is now entirely possible that people can live for some 20 years after retirement. This was not what the old age pension was designed for."

Understanding dawned over Daria and she nodded thoughtfully. Then she frowned slightly. "But, if you've paid taxes all your life, don't you think you should be entitled to receive a pension?" she asked.

Wise Owl nodded and said, "That is a common expectation that is constantly repeated, particularly by those who expect to receive a pension because they haven't prepared for their retirement.

"The thing to remember is that the taxes that were paid during a person's working life weren't put into a special fund just to be paid out to that person when they retire. Those taxes were used *at the time* for things that would benefit those people who were paying them, *at that time*.

"Things like schools, roads, bridges, airports, tunnels, hospitals, defence, people who were receiving pensions and welfare *at that time* and..." she paused and smiled, "politician's salaries and their benefits as well, which some people might say was money that was not well spent at all."

She continued, "But the money they expect to receive as a pension when they retire will be paid for by people who will be working *at that time*. And with the advances in modern medicine, some people may spend almost as much time receiving a pension as they spent working and paying taxes, while at the same time the pool of people working and paying taxes is shrinking.

"Governments have been slowly increasing or trying to increase the pension age because, in order to meet all their welfare commitments, they are relying on the next few generations to pay for this. But, as previously mentioned, in most developed countries the number of taxpayers has been decreasing due to the smaller subsequent generations.

"The birth rate of many countries has decreased to less than two children per family, which means you are not replacing each of the parents in the coming generation.

"Or what about a country that has a one-child policy? You effectively halve the population per generation if the policy is adopted for a long period. Not only are there less tax-paying workers to support the larger retiring generation, there is also a smaller consumer base to buy the goods and services produced.

"During the Baby Boom period, for every one person receiving government-funded welfare, there were at least five and as many as 16 people working and paying taxes, depending on where you lived. This figure has been reducing since that time.

"So now, in a new millennium, we will need to be smarter with our finances and start thinking of how we can help ourselves, rather than expecting our governments to help us. We need to look at ways of saving our money, reducing and eliminating our debts, investing and planning and saving for our own retirement."

Wise Owl paused, and then added, "It would be a very brave government indeed who will actually be proactive and substantially reduce or completely eliminate various welfare systems, especially the pension. I personally do not think the pension can ever be abolished."

"Can you imagine!" Daria exclaimed, "That government wouldn't last long."

"Well," Wise Owl asked, "Given our potentially long life spans, you need to ask yourself, what kind of existence would you expect on a wholly government-funded pension?"

Daria considered this. She thought of her grandparents who, while they had a mostly adequate retirement, theirs was a very frugal one, with very few holidays or luxuries and real concerns during emergencies. She thought of her parents who had no savings plan and who had put very little aside for their retirement and were expecting to receive a pension when they retired.

"A very basic one I suspect. Not a very good one anyway," she said at last.

Wise Owl nodded and said, "Consider this then. Statistically, in any given year, out of the average of one hundred 65 year olds:

- 25% are dead;
- 20% have well below average incomes, in other words below the poverty line;
- 51% have below to average incomes and this may be because some of them are still working;
- 4% have above average incomes; and
- 1 out of those 100 are millionaires.

"So what kind of retirement would you like to have?" she asked.

Daria thought about it for a moment. "Well, obviously the last four percent," she finally said.

Wise Owl nodded. "Yes, most people would prefer to be at that end rather than the other end. That's why you need to start financially educating yourself now.

"We'll go over an important step tomorrow. You need a vision or a goal. But don't worry, we are getting closer to how to establish your savings plan."

FINANCIALLY WISE ACTION PLAN –

Stop thinking that the company you work for or the government will provide for you. Start thinking about how you will provide for yourself and your family without any assistance. List 3 ways you could accomplish this.

Notes:

_____

_____

_____

_____

_____

4 WHAT IS YOUR VISION – YOUR WHY?

"If you were born without wings, do nothing to prevent them from growing."
Coco Chanel

[You can skip this section if you have already read this in one of the other books, although it is recommended that you reread these sections in each book. The stories may be different to fit in with the topic.]

"Right," said Wise Owl rubbing her hands together when they caught up the following day, "this lesson will be about why you want to have financial independence. Your whole reason for taking control of your finances."

Daria looked up expectantly.

Wise Owl continued, "This is probably the most important step in the whole process. You need a reason for wanting to save and achieve your financial independence. *Your vision of your future. Your "why"*. This might include things like:

- Your children
- Your retirement
- Your extended family
- Supplementing your job income and eventually leaving paid employment
- Leaving a legacy and creating family wealth
- Helping other people
- Making charitable contributions and setting up a charitable foundation
- Having more frequent and better holidays, homes and cars
- Anything at all that really moves you.

"This will be what motivates you to achieve financial freedom. It is not only everyone's right to achieve financial freedom, it is now our duty. As discussed earlier, our governments are rapidly approaching a time where they will not be able to adequately support us in our old age. We need to step up and take responsibility for this ourselves. After all, nobody has your own financial interests at heart as much as you do.

"Your 'why' determines your goals and overall vision. Your vision and goals should resonate with you. When you have a goal, you focus on it and you take action to move towards it. The actions you take, or your 'how', then become congruent with your vision which makes you more likely to commit to it. You are working hard to achieve a cause higher or greater than you."

"I have another story to share with you..." Wise Owl said.

Sumiko's family didn't have much when she was growing up. She never went without anything important – her parents made sure there was always enough for her and her sister – but real luxuries were rare.

Her parents believed very strongly in getting the best education possible for the girls and worked very hard to ensure that they went to the best schools, but it was apparent that Sumiko had been blessed with the brains in the family and consistently achieved excellent grades, while her sister struggled academically.

Sumiko went onto university and a career, while her sister married shortly after finishing high school. Her sister soon had a daughter, Akiko and then a son, Hiro, upon whom Sumiko doted as their aunt.

When Akiko started school, the family noticed she was having difficulty with simple tasks, and seemed to be regressing. After exhaustive testing, doctors finally diagnosed a brain tumour which was inoperable due to its position.

Sumiko was absolutely devastated and vowed to do all she could to help her niece. She started researching everything she could about Akiko's condition and spent a great deal of time and money on finding out as much as she could about possible cures.

She had considerable savings, which she used to travel to see various experts and get the best possible care and doctors for her niece. She also used a substantial amount of her savings to set up a charitable foundation to do more research on brain tumours.

"So you see, she had a cause greater than herself," said Wise Owl.

"Ooh," said Daria considering, "I have never actually connected what I earn with the bigger picture before. It's just been about getting paid, going out and spending it, waiting until next pay day, then going out and spending again. I see I need to give some thought and time to what I want."

"Yes," said Wise Owl. "Look at the bigger and overall picture of where you are going in your life. Your mindset is also a very important component of your financial journey. Henry Ford once said, 'Whether you think you can, or think you can't, you're right.' This is very true. Only you control your thoughts on what you believe you can achieve.

"Napoleon Hill also famously said 'Thoughts are things.' This is also true. All things we want for ourselves begin in our thoughts. In fact everything we can see or use around us was created twice. It first manifested itself in someone's thoughts before becoming something tangible.

"So, if we tell ourselves, 'I'm no good with money, it just seems to slip through my fingers' or 'I will never be able to afford a house' or 'I'm not smart enough to trade shares', then guess what? We're right! Whatever our thought patterns are around anything will magically come true, *because we believe it to be true*. We must use this knowledge to our advantage, not to our detriment."

"Yes," said Daria slowly, "I've always had those self-limiting beliefs about money."

Wise Owl nodded. "A lot of people do. They don't know any better. The key to this is education. Nobody is born an expert or has the knowledge already. Remember, there wasn't a winner who wasn't first a beginner. There are no failures, only lessons. We need to take control over, and become responsible for, all aspects of our finances.

"For example, there should be no need to cut up our credit cards if we take responsibility. A credit card is a very useful tool, for those who take responsibility. The danger lies not with the card itself, it is just a piece of plastic. The danger lies with the mindset that uses the card without taking responsibility for it."

Daria smiled, thinking of all the times she carelessly bought things on her credit card. The smile faded when she realised she never gave any thought to how she was going to repay it, assuming the minimum monthly payments would be sufficient.

Wise Owl caught her look of concern. She said "Don't think that you don't have an aptitude for money and finance. These are all learned skills and you can learn to develop your financial intelligence.

"Something many people get wrong is to mistake income for wealth. There are people earning very high incomes who hold far more debt than assets. There are also people who have never earned much year after year, but who have a very high net worth with businesses, property and share portfolios. It's not how much money you make, it's how much you keep and what you do with what you keep. Your real wealth is measured by your net worth – that is your total assets less your total liabilities.

"Your mindset will make all the difference to your financial situation, as it changes from a 'consumer' mindset into an 'investor' mindset."

Wise Owl pointed to Daria's pen poised expectantly over a new page in her notebook. She said, "Starting right now, you're going to write down your goals, short-term and long-term, and your vision of how you would like your life to be. Then write down your time frame when you'd like to achieve these. Be realistic. People often overestimate how much they can achieve in one year, but underestimate how much they can achieve in five or 10 years.

"Look for pictures of the things you'd like to have in your life. Cut them out or print them and put them onto your vision or notice board or scrapbook.

"Tomorrow we will look at your expenditure and the areas where you can make savings, but today, focus on you and what you want your life to look like."

Daria nodded "I'll get started on that straight away," she promised.

FINANCIALLY WISE ACTION PLAN –

Write down what you would like to achieve in your life, your wish list of what you would like to have and where you would like to be in one year, five years, 10 years and 20 years from now.

Pick four items from your one year list, whether an actual physical thing or an achievement. Write down a specific plan on how and when you will achieve each one in your allotted time frame.

Notes:

_____

_____

_____

_____

_____

_____

_____

5 FINDING YOUR HIDDEN CASH

"The safe way to double your money is to fold it over once and put it in your pocket."
Frank McKinney "Kin" Hubbard

[You can skip this section if you have already read this in one of the other books, although it is recommended that you reread these sections in each book. There is a more detailed section on specific savings in chapter 8.]

"Today's lesson is about looking at finding ways of cutting your expenditure and putting those funds towards saving," announced Wise Owl the following day. They were sitting on Daria's balcony overlooking the local park.

"Well," Daria said, "I'm pretty sure I don't waste my money on frivolous things." She paused, thinking. "Well, most of the time anyway," she added with a smile.

Wise Owl smiled back and said, "Well, we'll see. Most people seem to live to the very limit of their income, and think that a pay rise will solve all their problems.

"Everyone could do with some more cash. But you don't need to ask for a raise to generate more cash flow. In fact getting a raise is not the answer. Your spending always seems to go up in line with your pay rises. You are probably earning today an amount that a few years ago you were absolutely convinced would be the perfect amount of money you could live on, but you still find yourself struggling for cash."

She paused for a moment and then continued, "Sometimes it's the simple things you can do that make a difference. You have money hidden away and you don't even know it. If you didn't miss it before, you won't miss it now. You need to find your hidden money, which can then be channeled into savings. There are always ways of finding some spare cash, which can be put to better use."

Daria looked up from her notebook, where she had been busily writing today's lesson.

"I do try to be careful with my money, but somehow when I have money in my wallet, it seems to mysteriously disappear and get spent. For the life of me I can't figure out where it all went," she said.

Wise Owl agreed saying, "Believe me, you are not the only one to whom that happens. You need to monitor where it all goes. Firstly, track every single purchase you make for a month, especially the small things that you don't think about. That chocolate bar here, magazine there, the 3pm coffee to stay awake at work, the takeaway on the way home because it was too much trouble to cook that evening. These all add up.

"Think about how much you will earn in your entire working life. Think of how much you have already earned since you started working. How much of that do you still have? What do you have to show for what you have earned so far? What will you have to show for everything you expect to earn in your working lifetime? It's time to be smarter with your money," she continued.

"Let me share another story with you..."

Samantha lived with her boyfriend in a rented apartment, and felt it was time they started to save for their own home. They had trouble finding the extra money to put aside into their savings until they started to record where their money was actually going.

They were amazed to find how much all the small expenses here and there added up to a significant amount over time. Samantha decided that she could quite easily give up or reduce her fortnightly manicures and do her nails herself. Since it was also a social occasion with her girlfriends more than the actual manicure, they decided to meet in the park instead and take up walking. They still had the social interaction and were out and about getting exercise and fresh air. When it rained, they met at a local café. Her boyfriend decided he didn't need to catch up for a drink with the boys every Friday night, and cut it down to once or twice a month.

"I see the point you're making here," said Daria, "We're spending money without really thinking about it, without realising that all those small amounts can add up to large amounts if we're not careful."

"Exactly right!" exclaimed Wise Owl. "Until you really start to focus on that, you don't realise how those small amounts add up. Recording ALL the expenditure you make in a month can be a real eye opener. You'll be amazed to see where your cash just gets frittered away."

Daria guiltily recalled when she had last filled her car with fuel and bought a chocolate bar because it was at the counter. Then there was the magazine she had bought at the supermarket because she was leafing through it at the checkout and she wanted to finish the article she was reading. But then she also remembered that a number of people in the queue in front of her at both the service station and supermarket had done exactly the same thing and she realised the placement of these items was deliberate, to encourage impulse buys.

Wise Owl continued, "Here are just a few things to get you started:

- Firstly, try to use cash rather than putting it on a credit or charge card. Psychology shows it's harder to hand over cash than to simply put it on a card, where you don't actually see your physical money diminishing or disappearing.
- Instead of spending the coins you receive as change, put them into a money box or jar and when full, deposit this into your savings account.
- Make your lunch at home and bring it in to work at least a couple of times a week instead of buying it every day.
- Buy a jar of nice coffee or a packet of ground coffee and a single cup coffee plunger to keep in your drawer at work, rather than purchasing a takeaway coffee. The added benefit here is that you'll use your own mug instead of throwing away a single use cardboard coffee cup."

Daria was scribbling furiously in her pad. Wise Owl was on a roll now.

- "There are obvious ones like quit smoking if you're a smoker and cut down on your alcohol purchases. Double benefit again, your health improves as well as your hip pocket.
- Walk that short distance instead of taking the car.
- Take a few minutes before shopping to plan your meals so you won't be tempted to buy takeaways or unnecessary items. Buy only what you need. If you go with a shopping list you're less likely to put those impulse things into your trolley.
- Don't go shopping when you're hungry. You're less likely to put snack products into your trolley.

- Drink water instead of buying sugary soft drinks, sodas or pop. There's that health and financial benefit thing again.
- Prepare for bills in advance and always pay them on time. Not only will you not incur late fees and/or interest charges, you'll create or keep a good credit rating."

She paused for a moment. "That reminds me of a story about a friend and her run in with her telephone company..."

Andrea had always paid her phone bill on time; however one month her phone was accidentally cut off by the phone company (the company had the incorrect phone number details).

When she was finally reconnected and received her next bill, she was extremely displeased to find that she had been charged a connection fee. She rang the company and asked for it to be removed. They assured her it would be and that she should pay the amount without the connection fee, which she did.

The following bill had not only the outstanding connection fee on it, but interest charges for overdue amounts. She rang the company again and they again told her to pay just the new charges without the connection fee and interest charges. Again she followed their suggestion.

When she received the next bill not only did it still have the connection fee and original interest, it also had additional interest charges. She rang the company and told them she was absolutely not going to pay their invoice and she was changing phone suppliers.

She changed phone company but still had a few months going backward and forward with the old phone company over the charges. After receiving some legal letters she eventually paid the outstanding amount less the connection fee and interest charges (which the phone company finally cancelled), and thought no more about it.

She was therefore horrified to find, after applying for a car loan some time later, that she had a black mark against her credit rating from the phone company. Was the phone company in the wrong? Yes. However Andrea was also in the wrong by not paying the charges that were due, and it impacted on her when she least needed it.

"I'd never really placed a lot of value or thought on my credit rating," admitted Daria.

"People don't. Until they need it. But because they didn't know, by the time they find out it might be too late. Information about your credit rating is easy to obtain and it's a good idea to check it every couple of years." Wise Owl said.

"This brings me to my next point. Our need for more 'things', for the latest and greatest and trying to 'keep up with the Joneses'. You don't really need to rush out and get the latest gizmo, gadget or doodad when the one you have now is just fine. Repair or replace it when you need to, don't buy things because you want to impress people.

"Work out your hourly rate if you don't already know it. Then work out how long you would have to work to buy a particular item. Some items may only require an hour or less. But some other items might require many hours or days of work, at your hourly rate, to pay for it. Once you realise the true cost of something, in terms of how many hours you need to work to pay for it, you may decide you don't want it that badly after all. Or perhaps the money could be put to better use. That is the opportunity cost of using the money for one purpose over another.

"In Thomas Stanley and William Danko's book, The Millionaire Next Door, they found that most millionaires lived modestly and frugally, drove older cars, flew economy class and lived well within their means. Will Smith has been attributed with saying, 'Too many people spend money they haven't earned, buying things they don't want, to impress people they don't like.' I might add 'with money they don't have.' Don't go into debt to impress someone else who in all probability doesn't even care. Whether Will Smith actually said that or not doesn't matter, it's the sentiment behind the statement that should resonate."

"Well, at least the Smiths don't try to keep up with the Joneses," quipped Daria.

Wise Owl laughed and then continued, "It's not just things we buy, it's things we already have. Another area to look at is to go through your 'stuff'. Everyone has things they no longer need or use. Look through every room in your house, from your bedroom wardrobe to your kitchen cupboards and especially your garage.

"Now, consider selling these items or having a garage sale. Investigate selling sites like eBay and your local area sell pages on Facebook to list your items or just advertise in your local paper. One person's junk is another person's treasure, so it's a double benefit. And the fact that you're also de-cluttering is a triple benefit. But don't fill the newly available space with more 'stuff' – this defeats the whole purpose of the exercise."

Daria smiled thinking about the times she had gone through her wardrobe to find things she could donate or give away. It was not that she no longer wore the item in question, it was because she needed the room for the new items she had bought.

"Ok," she said nodding, "I fully see where you're coming from about unnecessary expenditure on things you don't need, and I'll never do that again. I promise!" she exclaimed.

Wise Owl laughed and said, "I'm not advocating being a miser and never spending on anything other than essentials. You do need to reward yourself with an occasional treat every now and then, but the key word here is *occasional*. If you see something you must have, I suggest you try this to gauge how much you really want it. Leave it for a day. Sleep on it. Put it out of your mind. If you still really want the item and it's a must have, then you know it is something you will appreciate and is not just an impulse buy that you might regret later on. By all means buy it."

"There are so many things to consider here, the ways to save money can fill many books, but start thinking about areas where YOU can save money, and if you start by recording every single purchase for a month, even that packet of chewing gum, this will make it much easier when you do a budget later and you'll be well on your way to taking control of your finances."

Wise Owl ended, "I think that's probably enough for today. Tomorrow we'll briefly go over the people who will help you and the importance of having a team around you."

FINANCIALLY WISE ACTION PLAN –

Become conscious of where your money is going every day.

Keep track of all your expenditure for at least one month by writing it down, whether it is in a notebook or a spreadsheet. When out, keep all your receipts and write on them what the purchase was for so they can be recorded.

At the end of the month, list three items or areas where you could reduce your spending. Add this money to your savings.

For your own interest, calculate how much you might expect to earn in your entire working life. Calculate 10 percent of this figure, which is what you could have in savings (in today's money).

Notes:

6 YOUR TEAM

"Alone we can do so little; together we can do so much."
Helen Keller

[You can skip this section if you have already read this in one of the other books, although it is recommended that you reread these sections in each book. There are suggested resources at the back of the book.]

Wise Owl and Daria were sitting in Daria's lounge room on a rainy afternoon after a delicious high tea.

"I want to very quickly discuss an important aspect that many people don't take into account. It's the importance of having a good team around you to help you achieve your goals." began Wise Owl taking a last sip of her tea before setting the cup down into the saucer.

Daria looked enquiringly at Wise Owl and raised her eyebrows.

"Do I need to save with someone else, as a member of a team?" she asked.

"No, no," laughed Wise Owl, "What I mean is that you need to have experienced and knowledgeable people around you who are able to provide you with good advice. They will help you assess whether an investment, or something you are looking at doing, is a good idea and can point out potential pitfalls and traps. They can look at things with a fresh perspective and provide you with a different point of view. Something you may not have thought about. They can also help to keep you accountable to your goals.

"Napoleon Hill talked about the power of the Master Mind principle in his book 'Think and Grow Rich'. This is the group of people with whom you might consult before making a decision. They usually have areas of expertise that can complement your skills and knowledge." she continued.

"You might not require this expertise just yet. You're at the start of your financial journey. But you won't be able to do everything by yourself, and if you start to develop your network now, you'll be ready to take advantage of opportunities that may present themselves in the future." she concluded.

"Oh, I see." said Daria thoughtfully. "So I'm looking for people who can help me with my vision, goals and ideas and advise me when I need some expert knowledge." She paused for a moment and then asked, "Who should I have on my team?"

"Well, let me think," said Wise Owl. "I'll tell you a story about a friend of mine who needed a new car because her old one desperately needed replacing, but she didn't have any savings, so her friend and mentor started to teach her financial skills."

"That sounds familiar…" began Daria "Oh!" she exclaimed in understanding. "You're a member of my team. My first member."

Yes! You have me for a start." nodded Wise Owl.

"I do, don't I." said Daria with a laugh. "You mentioned Team Daria earlier. I'm already developing my team."

"Yes indeed." said Wise Owl. "I'm here to help you in the capacity of adviser and mentor. But some other important people you might like to consider for your team, depending on what you are planning to do, might include:

- An accountant or bookkeeper.
- Lawyer, solicitor or legal adviser.
- Banker or finance expert.
- Real estate strategist.
- Finance or mortgage broker.
- Stockbroker or stock adviser.
- Insurance broker
- Financial planner.
- Venture capitalist or angel investor.
- Business coaches.
- Other mentors."

"You mean other people to mentor me, not just you?" Daria asked, intrigued.

"Of course," Wise Owl said nodding. "I might not have the specific knowledge or experience in a particular area that you're looking for. You might want to grow beyond what I've taught you or you're looking for a different set of skills. There's a saying that when the student is ready, the teacher will appear.

"What's more, you don't necessarily have to meet in person whichever mentor or mentors you choose. You can learn from some of the greats through other means, such as:

- reading their books or reading books about them;
- listening to their CDs and podcasts;
- watching their DVDs;
- attending their seminars, doing their programs and hearing them speak when they happen to be in town;
- connecting with them through their website or social media;
- subscribing to their mailing lists;
- attending their webinars;

- reading their newsletters or reading about them, or interviews with them, in periodicals, journals, newspapers or magazines.
- or simply writing them a letter or email.

"Isaac Newton purportedly called it standing on the shoulders of giants to help him see further. You're getting their wisdom and knowledge and benefitting from their experience without having to do all the hard work again by yourself."

"Oh, wow." said Daria with a faraway look in her eye. "You're right, I can learn from the best minds without having to start by myself from the beginning. Whatever I want to do, when I'm ready to take that step, I'm quite sure someone has already done it, and I can hear or read their account and not make the same mistakes."

"That's exactly right." beamed Wise Owl. "There are whole libraries with every kind of information you could ever want and need. You might want to build your own library of information and inspiring reading and listening. But perhaps start by looking at what's available in your local library and browsing through your local bookstore or even have a look through Amazon's catalogues."

"Remember though," she cautioned, "you are wanting to obtain as much advice and information as you can on a particular course of action that you want to take, so you can make a decision. You're not handing over the decision making to someone else. The object is always for you to take control of your own financial wellbeing.

"But you need to make informed choices and decisions. There could be legal or financial or taxation implications in a particular course of action that you're thinking of taking. You need to know all the possible scenarios and consequences of taking that action.

"For example, your accountant can advise you of the best structure into which to purchase an asset to minimise your potential liability and taxes. Your lawyer can advise you on any contracts you might sign. Your banker could advise you on a low or high interest account you could use, depending on your purpose. Your real estate strategist might advise you on the growth potential of the area in which you're looking to buy and your stockbroker might be able to advise you on upcoming stock floats from which you could benefit.

"Ultimately, you are the one who has to make the decision. It's you who is risking your money, but if you have all the correct and unbiased knowledge and information at hand, you can make the right decision for you."

Wise Owl paused considering, "This means you need to be careful from whom you do take advice. It needs to be impartial and independent and the adviser should not benefit from you taking a particular course of action." she concluded.

Noticing Daria's increasingly concerned look she said encouragingly, "Don't worry too much about all that until you are ready to take your investing to the next level. You are just starting out now and it's all still new to you.

"As you further your education through the various channels we discussed earlier, your knowledge will increase and you will be able to make many informed decisions and choices yourself. You will have a much greater understanding of the advice that is given to you and be able to ask educated questions.

"Right now, you just need to understand that you could probably not achieve a great deal without your Master Mind team to help you. It's been said that if you're the smartest person in the room, you're in the wrong room. You need to surround yourself with people who have the complementary skills, knowledge and abilities to help you achieve your goals. You can find people right now with whom you might form strategic partnerships and joint ventures in the future. It's not just their experience and knowledge you can access. With the right team you could also utilise their time, money and ideas. They'll also make sure that you do what you say you're going to do. And one day you might find yourself being a mentor to others as you gain more knowledge and wisdom.

"But for the moment just start thinking about your strategy and start looking for people you could add to your team." Wise Owl stopped and looked at her watch.

She looked across to Daria and smiled. "We're now getting to the good stuff. Tomorrow's lesson will be about putting the savings plan into action."

Daria nodded enthusiastically, "I'm looking forward to it."

FINANCIALLY WISE ACTION PLAN –

Think about how many people you meet every day and over the course of a week, month or year. Any of the people you meet could potentially be your next mentor, advisor, business partner or even a mentee. Start to network and look for potential team members.

These are initially the people you might meet through every day interaction and also at seminars and events. They should complement the skills you have by providing knowledge or expertise in areas in which you might not be familiar. You may also find potential partners for joint ventures.

Ideally you are looking for a synergistic relationship which would be mutually beneficial to everyone.

Notes:

_____

_____

_____

_____

_____

7 PUTTING A SAVINGS PLAN INTO ACTION

"Compound interest is the eighth wonder of the world. She who understands it, earns it... she who doesn't... pays it."
(With apologies to) Albert Einstein

"Right," said Wise Owl briskly, when she met up with Daria for the next lesson. "We will now get down to the actual nuts and bolts of getting your savings plan underway."

Daria looked up expectantly, her pen at the ready hovering over a new page on her pad. They were sitting at her kitchen table after an early breakfast.

Wise Owl began, "The easiest way to start saving is to have this happen automatically without any input required. Firstly, open a completely separate account as your designated 'savings' account. This can be any type of savings account, but preferably one that can't be easily accessed, such as an online account, or one that penalises you with a lower or no interest for withdrawals."

Daria nodded seeing the logic of this. She remembered an advertisement she'd seen recently from a virtual bank that offered good interest rates, but did not actually have a bricks and mortar branch or automatic teller machines to provide temptation. It was all online. She would investigate further.

Wise Owl continued, "Next, set up an automatic transfer to move a set amount from your regular 'working' account into this account. Alternatively you might be able to speak with your payroll department to have them pay your salary into two accounts: your regular and your savings account. This is a very basic and easy form of wealth creation to implement. It is called 'Paying yourself first'."

"Yes, you mentioned that before, paying myself first. But isn't that what I do now?" queried Daria. "The money I earn gets paid directly to me." She frowned, looking puzzled.

"Do you? Is it?" asked Wise Owl. "If you paid yourself first, you'd have a substantial amount in savings. Who do you really pay first?" she asked. "Is it really yourself, or is it your landlord or your bank, your electricity and gas provider, your phone provider, your local supermarket and service station, your local clothes shops, fast food outlets and restaurants? I could go on, but you get where I'm going.

"No, what I mean by paying yourself first is that as soon as you receive your pay, or any income for that matter, you take a percentage of what you have received and put it aside either into a savings account or investment. You then use the remainder of what's left to pay your bills, food and entertainment.

"Most people pay everyone else first and then try and pay themselves with what's left. Invariably, there's nothing left, which is why people say there's too much month left at the end of money. They're waiting for the next pay day because they've run out of money.

"But aren't you the most important person in your life? Shouldn't you be paid first? Don't you deserve to be the first person on your list to receive payment?

"Let me share a story with you to illustrate..."

Bridget wanted to join her friends on a yearlong overseas holiday that was planned to be their adventure of a lifetime – travelling the world while they were young and single. The holiday was planned in two years' time, to give them enough time to save the necessary amount to cover airfares, accommodation and likely expenses.

Bridget immediately ran into problems when she tried to leave some money in her account after every pay cycle. She found that her expenditure always managed to match exactly what happened to be left in her account. She was paying all her bills and expenses, and then trying to save with whatever was left, which was usually nothing.

Once she realised the importance of paying herself first, and paying everyone else with what was left, she set up a new Internet account with a bank that didn't have a local branch. She then went online to her usual bank account (the one her salary was paid into and her bills were paid from) and set up an automatic bank transfer to move a set amount of 10% of her pay into her special 'holiday' Internet account every payday.

As she wasn't seeing this money in her account, because the money was moved out immediately, she soon found that she didn't even miss it. She further found that she could actually still manage to pay her bills and meet her expenses with what was left. She also started actively looking for ways to cut down on her day-to-day costs. She increased the amount of the transfer to 15% after six months, and then to 20% only five months after that. She managed to save more than enough to cover airfares and accommodation for her holidays. If she had any holiday jobs, she tried to have her wages paid into her 'holiday' account whenever possible.

Once she returned home from her holiday of a lifetime, which had turned into an 18-month adventure, she secured a good job and continued her savings regime of always paying herself first.

"So Daria," said Wise Owl. "Robert Kiyosaki in his book 'Rich Dad Poor Dad' says you should have your money work hard for you, rather than you work hard for money. Is your money working hard for you, or are you working hard for money?"

Light dawned on Daria's face. "Yes!" she exclaimed. "I've been doing it the wrong way around. I am the most important person in my life and I deserve to be paid first. And my money should be working for me, rather than me working for money. Always chasing after money." She was quiet for a moment.

"So...," she queried "how much should I be paying myself then, or in other words, putting into my savings account?".

"Well," said Wise Owl, "It's completely up to you! A good rule of thumb is ten per cent of your income, like in the example, but you can change this figure to suit yourself. Ten per cent might be a bit much to begin with, so start with whatever you're comfortable with. Start with one per cent if that's all you can afford, but try to increase that when you can. You just need to start. And remember, income isn't just your regular earned income. Don't forget to save ten percent of:

- overtime
- bonuses
- tax returns
- cash gifts
- business or investment income, dividends and interest
- winnings from lotteries or gambling
- basically any extra money you receive.

Daria was scribbling furiously in her notepad.

"Alternatively, you can save a fixed amount periodically, be it weekly, fortnightly or monthly. The same amount goes to your savings on a regular basis and it builds up that way." Wise Owl continued.

"Let compound interest work to your advantage. Albert Einstein reportedly called compound interest the eighth wonder of the world. This is when you start earning interest on your previously earned interest. The longer you are able to take advantage of compound interest, the more dramatic your returns."

Wise Owl said, "Let me draw you a chart on how compound interest works."

She took Daria's notebook and pen.

"Let's start with a figure of 1,000 and assume it increases at 3% interest per year for 20 years."

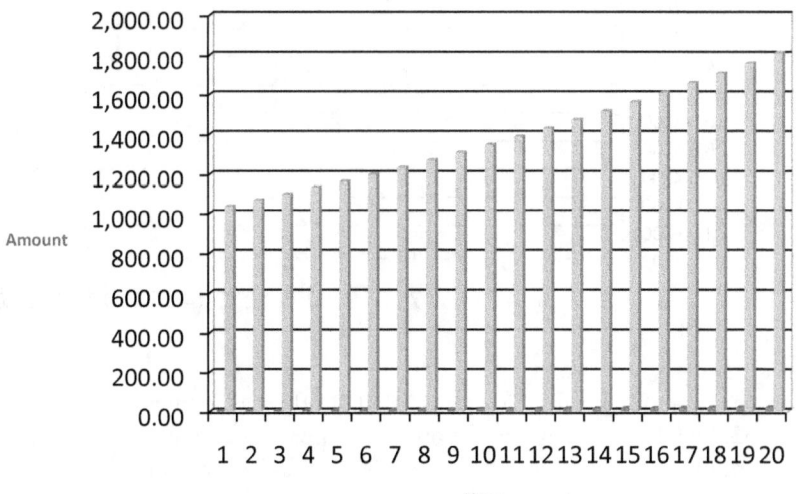

She passed the notebook and pen back to Daria.

Wise Owl said, "For your savings, this is a set and forget strategy. Just doing nothing has almost doubled your money. That's the miracle of compound interest. This is good if you unexpectedly come into some money and you set it aside for a rainy day. It works best over a very long period of time as eventually the interest amount becomes greater than the initial amount and it grows exponentially."

Wise Owl continued, "But look what happens when you add an extra 100 per month, or 1,200 per year, to the initial 1,000 over the same time period and assume a 3% return."

And she took Daria's notebook and pen again and drew another diagram in it before handing it back.

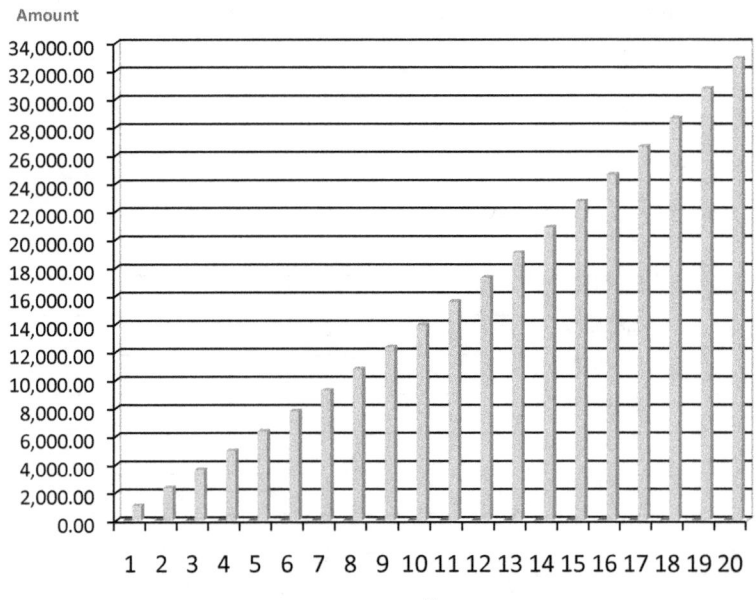

Wise Owl said "You see that 1,000 has turned into nearly 33,000! Now, imagine if you could get more than 3%? Or you could get 3% monthly, quarterly or half yearly instead of per annum? This is the miracle of a regular savings plan."

[Note: these are very simplistic representations of compound interest and do not take all factors into account, e.g., interest calculated daily has a more positive effect than interest calculated monthly or yearly and inflation and taxes can also impact on returns.]

Daria was impressed. "Yes, I see how that works. It's better over a longer period though." She sighed. "I wish I'd started saving as a child. My parents didn't really open savings accounts for us. They just didn't know. I could have so much more now, even though I wasn't earning all that much when I got my first job." She was silent for a moment, lost in thought.

"Well," said Wise Owl, "The point is it doesn't matter when you start saving or how much you save, what matters is that you start and it's never too early or too late to start. And as I've said previously, how much you earn has no bearing on your ability to save either. Someone on a minimum wage could manage to put aside significant savings, while another person earning six figures annually could have a huge amount of debt and absolutely no savings. It really isn't about how much you earn. It's all about how much you keep, and what you do with what you keep. Remember, your wealth is calculated by your net worth.

"Eventually you would ideally have a number of savings accounts for which you could set up automatic transfers. For example, one for consumable items, such as cars, holidays and television sets, and one you might like to call your 'wealth account' for investing and wealth building. You can have as many savings accounts as you want. There's no limit on how many you can have, provided your accounts have no or very low fees. Just make sure you do your homework and select your bank or banks carefully. Your savings accounts do not all need to be with the same bank.

"Let me share another example with you..."

Lisa moved into her first shared accommodation with two other girls after she obtained her first job. She didn't have much money and was trying to put together some furniture items, but had been given an old analogue television set by her cousin when he upgraded to a nice new larger sized digital one. It had pride of place in their lounge room and was used by them all, not just to watch their favourite shows, but they also rented new-release movies and invited friends over for movie nights, since it was much cheaper than going to the cinema.

Then they found out that the analogue signal in their area was going to be switched off in 18 months. Lisa didn't want to take out a loan and go into debt, so decided she would save up for a new television set. She did some research and found a good brand and approximate pricing. She gave herself 12 months to save for this new television set. She worked out how much she would need to save each pay into her newly opened savings account in order to reach the total amount.

With an unexpected pay rise due to an internal promotion, she managed to save the required amount in ten months. When she shopped around, she managed to get a much better and larger model, not just because the technology had improved and costs had gone down in that short time, but also because she was paying in cash, which gave her better bargaining power.

Wise Owl turned to Daria. "The foundation of achieving your financial goals is firstly to become disciplined with your savings, as this becomes the basis for increasing your financial assets.

"You should always try to have some funds in savings, but don't become complacent. Due to the effects of inflation and taxation, you may not always be breaking even, let alone getting ahead. Therefore conduct an annual review of all your investments, including your savings accounts, to make sure your money is still working for you."

Wise Owl smiled. "I do believe you are ready to become a fully-fledged member of the savings club. Your education on savings is pretty much complete. Now it's up to you."

Daria jumped up, excited by the prospect and what the future held. "I'm ready." she said.

FINANCIALLY WISE ACTION PLAN –

Set up a regular automatic transfer of the amount you have chosen to save from your working, everyday bank account to your special high interest, low fee savings account.

Review this amount at least once or twice a year and make sure you put the dates for these reviews in your calendar. Increase the amount if and when you can.

Sit back and watch your savings grow. Look at paying off debts. Start to investigate investment options.

Notes:

_____

_____

_____

_____

_____

_____

8 MONEY SAVING AREAS

"A penny saved is a penny gained"
English Proverb

Daria and Sage met up a few weeks later for lunch.

"So, how is it all going for you?" Sage asked Daria.

"Well," began Daria, "I've set up my savings account. Or rather, accounts." She beamed at Sage. "Yep, I decided I could do with two accounts: one for future investments and one for my new car. I'm putting ten per cent of everything I earn into each account."

"Oh, well done, I'm so proud of you!" exclaimed Sage.

Daria smiled and nodded. "I'm proud of me too. I just wish there was a way of boosting my savings without compromising my lifestyle too much."

Sage replied, "There are so many ways of saving money, all of which you can then redirect into your savings. It's quite possible you won't even miss most of these things while doing so. Let's go through some of these right now."

"All right, I'm ready," said Daria after fishing out her notebook and pen from her bag.

NOTE: Some of these may not be applicable to you, your situation or may not be available where you live. This is just a general, and by no means exhaustive, list. It is just to get you thinking. I'm sure after you have a look through this list, you'll be able to come up with many of your own examples.

Food, Groceries and Shopping

We have already mentioned a few things to look out for, such as resisting buying those extra high-profit-margin items located at the supermarket checkout or when filling your car up with fuel.

Make no mistake, the layout of supermarkets, shops and particularly the checkout areas is a science. They are designed for maximum expenditure from you, the consumer. The arrangement of the aisles is no accident either and the fact that staples such as fruit, vegetables, bread and milk are usually at opposite ends of the supermarket is so that you are almost forced to pass every aisle.

This, along with the smell of freshly baked bread and music playing in the background to relax you and encourage you to take your time, is deliberate so you can put more items in your trolley. Don't believe claims that advertising doesn't work. If it didn't work it wouldn't be such a lucrative industry with billions spent annually.

But you can play the game at your level, not their level. Below are some simple time tested things you can do to keep you from slipping into temptation.

Food – Shopping

- Plan your meals in advance and make a list.
- Make sure you're not hungry or tired when you go shopping. You'll be less tempted to put snack foods or sugary drinks in your trolley.
- Use a small trolley or basket rather than a large trolley.
- Some supermarkets, butchers, bakers and greengrocers will often have food and produce at reduced prices at the end of the day or just before closing. Some restaurants, other food outlets and farmers markets do this as well. They don't then have to carry it over to the next day or bring it back home with them and are happy to sell it cheaply just to get rid of it.
- Make sure you check out what's on special at your local shops. There's always a sale on somewhere.
- Look in your pantry. Do you have a number of ingredients in there already that can be made into several meals with just a couple of items from the supermarket? A packet of pasta, cheese, herbs and a tin of tuna can go a long way and make a great meal or meals.
- Make double or more portions and freeze the rest, so on those days you come home late or you just don't feel like cooking, there's already a homemade meal in the freezer. No need to get takeaway!
- Also, don't forget to actually look in your refrigerator as well. Most households throw away a tremendous amount of food every year because it's been in the fridge too long or it's past its 'use by' or 'best before' date. This should not happen once you start planning your meals.

When shopping:

- Compare the unit cost per weight of the same or similar items. The bigger box or weight is not necessarily the cheapest. However, buying in bulk for items you know you will definitely use can save you heaps of money. Consider joining buying clubs or warehouse stores, such as Costco, or cash and carry stores.
- Buy fruit and vegetables that are in season and preferably locally grown. While it's nice to be able to have different kinds of fruit and vegetables all year around, some of these have travelled halfway across the world and come with considerable 'food miles' and associated costs. Do your hip pocket and the environment a favour – visit your local fruit and vegetable wholesale markets, farmers' markets and co-ops.

Food – Grow Your Own

Consider growing some of your own food. This can be done even if you live in an apartment or flat, although it does help if there is a balcony. You just need a sunny position and a few pots or Styrofoam boxes.

Some fruit and vegetables are very easy to grow, such as:
- Root vegetables like carrots, beets, turnips, potatoes, etc.
- Tomatoes

- Strawberries
- Herbs can be grown in small pots on the kitchen bench, where they can be used as required. Dry surplus herbs for future use.
    o Your home grown food can be pickled or preserved for later use, and whether fresh or preserved, make great gifts to give to people.
    o Plant extra herbs in pretty pots to give as gifts.
    o Sell any surplus you have grown.
    o See if your area has a local produce "swap" meet where you can exchange food you've grown with food grown by someone else.

If you have children, have them involved with the garden. There's no bigger incentive for children than to eat something they've grown themselves, and it's certainly one way of having them eat their vegetables.

Food – Making

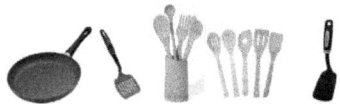

Try getting together once a week or fortnight with some friends who have their own favourite recipes. Everyone cooks big batches of their own special meals and you all split it amongst each other, so you have something different for dinner rather than your own well-used recipes.

Make it a fun and social event. Get together at a friend's house and rotate the venue if that's practical. Otherwise, just spend one day, or even an afternoon cooking up a storm.

If you have children, have them pitch in and help. The benefit here is that the children, both boys and girls, will learn to cook, which will be extremely handy for them when the time comes for them to move out on their own. They'll get home-cooked meals and they can also be creative and suggest different dishes to try.

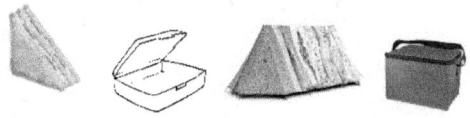

While on that topic, how about bringing your own lunch to work instead of going out and buying it? When you buy your lunch from a shop, you are not just paying for the food, you're also paying for the rent, staff wages, electricity, gas and other expenses incurred by the business. You don't have to make your own lunch every day, try it for one day a week to begin with and gradually increase the number of days you make your lunch instead of buying it. It can be as easy as leftovers from the night before.

Most workplaces have refrigerators and microwaves and even sandwich toasters. Make use of the company's kitchen freezer attached to the refrigerator to store leftovers. This can be very handy if you've cooked a lot of meals, but don't have enough room in your own freezer to store it all. It does make it a bit difficult if these are not provided by the company you work for; however, not all your lunches may require refrigeration or heating, and you could use an insulated bag for sandwiches and salads.

Shopping - Extras

Do you like to buy a morning or afternoon coffee every day? Or at least every workday? Work out the cost of your weekly takeaway coffees, and then multiply that by the number of weeks you work during the year. Imagine saving or contributing at least some of that amount towards your debts instead!

Add up the cost of all the magazines you buy weekly or monthly. There is a reason magazines are conveniently located at the checkout. They are little impulse buys for people stuck in a queue. Do you really need to buy all those magazines? Your local library is a good source of practically all magazines issued, as well as newspapers and, if required, they also have photocopiers for those articles you really want to keep and read again.

Shopping - Clothing

Do you love to buy clothes and shoes? Probably a silly question. But there is a serious side to this question. Being well dressed doesn't have to cost a lot.

- Have a few staple items in your wardrobe that you can turn into several outfits.
- Look at outlets to get end of line and end of season clothing and footwear. If you buy shrewdly and get classic looks, the items can be worn for many seasons.
- It can be cheaper to buy winter clothes in summer and summer clothes in winter. Look at stocking up next year's wardrobe during the end of season sales.
- Does every item of clothing you buy have to be new? Have you considered browsing through opportunity (op), charity or thrift shops? There are literally millions of items donated every year to these shops who then sell them at a fraction of their original cost. And they are likely to be good quality and often designer brand names. Try clothing "swap" meets to get exchange your old clothes for something different.
- If you have, or have access to, a sewing machine, you could make your own clothes or repurpose old clothes.

Motor Vehicle

Your motor vehicle, whatever it might be from scooter to car to something larger, is a money pit. Don't be fooled by your bank or other institutions that list your motor vehicle as an asset. An asset is something that pays you money. Motor vehicles cost you money.

Even a vintage or classic car that might appreciate in value will still require insurance at the very least if you don't drive it and will also require fuel, oil and maintenance if you do.

Something to remember is that an appreciating asset is worth the market value only if it is actually realised. In other words, only when an asset is sold and exchanged for cash can its value be determined. What goes up in value can also go down in value.

Consider these alternatives rather than owning your own car:

- Using taxis can be cheaper than the total expense of owning a car, when fuel, insurance, registration, repairs and maintenance are factored in.
- Using services such as Uber and Lyft or their equivalent can be even cheaper.
- Using public transport is probably even cheaper still.

It is, however, sometimes difficult to live without a motor vehicle of some sort, and there are ways in which you can save money on motor vehicle expenditure.

Let's start with the actual purchase of the vehicle. There are times during the month and the year and even the time of day when you can get very good deals on motor vehicles.

Firstly, decide on the make and model and also age if you're looking for a second-hand vehicle. Then:

- Do some research on all the sellers in your area and make quick visits to scope out their stock, availability and pricing.
- Know how much you're willing to pay for your preferred make and model. For a second-hand car, there are a number of web sites that can give you

- indicative pricing based on the make, model, year, odometer reading and general condition.
- Buying privately can save you significant amounts, but always remember the caveat emptor (buyer beware) clause. Always do your checks on the car's ownership and mechanicals.
- Become a member of local auto clubs that can do motor vehicle inspections and provide information if you don't have the expertise or know someone you trust who can help you.

Good times to buy and bargain include:

- At the end of the month, when the salesperson is trying to meet their monthly quota.
- The end of the financial year, when the dealership is trying to meet its annual quota.
- Annual or half yearly sales.
- End of model run outs, when a newer model is about to be announced and you can get the current models at reduced prices.
- Demonstrator models, that is, vehicles that were used for customers to test drive.
- Also, try and get into the dealership at the beginning or towards the end of the day of a weekday rather than a weekend, as there are likely to be less customers competing for salespeople and you will be more likely to have their undivided attention.
- If the salesperson is not able to drop their price significantly, they may be able to throw in free extras and upgrades.

If you don't think you can bargain effectively or negotiate the best deal, consider using a motor vehicle broker or buying agent. If you have a make, model and price, consult with a broker to see if they might be able to get you a better deal.

Also, if you travel a lot for your work, consider if a lease might be a better and cheaper option. Make sure you do your sums though, to ensure you will actually save money.

Once you have your vehicle:

- Service it regularly and to the manufacturer's specifications (this is usually a condition of your manufacturer's warranty). Budget for this to occur at regular intervals at a modest cost and it will save you from large and unexpected expenses in the future. Many new cars offer fixed price servicing over a period of time, so you know now much to budget for. Do not skimp on this expense. The last thing you want to happen is to break down in an isolated spot late at night. Perform some basic checks yourself, such as keeping tyres correctly inflated, regularly checking the oil, water, brake fluid and transmission fluid levels.

- Learn your local area's fuel cycles. The price of oil fluctuates and ultimately determines the price of your fuel. However, there are times when fuel prices are cheaper, usually one day during the week. Don't drive further than usual to find cheaper fuel though. This is not cost effective if you've used more fuel to get to and from the service station to begin with. Also be aware that many fuel stations increase prices dramatically before and during public holidays and long weekend holidays. Remove any unnecessary items from your car as the extra weight uses more fuel.

- Do you even need to take the car? The majority of fuel is used at engine start up, especially if only travelling a short distance.

- Could you walk there instead?
- Could you cycle there?
- Use the car when you have a number of errands and do them all in one go, travelling from one place or appointment to the next.
- Let your children walk to and from school, even if only a couple of times a week. Walk with them if you can. Only drop them off if you're actually driving somewhere anyway.
- Consider carpooling with other people from your work who live nearby or carpool with friends or neighbours who work in the same area. Park centrally and everyone contributes to parking and fuel costs, or alternate cars between the car owners.
- Use public transport wherever possible and walk to the nearest train station, bus, tram or ferry stop.

Your wallet and your health will benefit.

Banks

You need to investigate your bank as much as you investigate any other expense.

Be aware of the fees your bank charges. They might be offering high interest on your savings account, but they may be recouping this by charging high fees on your accounts. Make sure you audit your bank to ensure you are still receiving the best deal with regard to fees and interest. Be prepared to walk away from your bank if you don't get better service. If you don't really want to go through the hassle of changing banks, speak with your bank about removing fees or receiving a better interest rate. Make your bank work for your money and business!

When using an automatic teller machine (ATM), find out if you will be charged for making withdrawals and how much. Many banks charge fees if you use an ATM from another bank. There are also private ATMs that charge everyone who use them a fee. Those "holes in the wall" are handy and easily accessible, but banks and private ATM suppliers rely on this convenience and charge accordingly. These fees soon add up.

Mortgage

If you have a mortgage, know what your current interest rate is, and also what other banks' interest rates are. As with your bank account, audit your mortgage and see if it is still the best for your circumstances. If you find a better deal, think about changing your mortgage provider or approach your bank and ask either to match or even better the deal.

Also, consider using offset accounts to use your incoming pay to reduce your mortgage every pay cycle. An offset account is an account attached to your mortgage into which you deposit your pay and any other income. This then reduces your total mortgage amount by whatever balance is in your offset account. Try to leave that money in there for as long as possible before drawing any out.

Making more frequent payments rather than the standard monthly payment, e.g. fortnightly or weekly, will significantly reduce the term of the mortgage, as will any extra payments.

Credit Cards

Credit cards can be an incredibly useful, handy and beneficial tool or a burden, depending on how you use them. There's no need to cut up your credit card if you can master it and show restraint. Obviously the ideal situation would be to use your credit card wisely and pay it off in full every month. If this is not yet possible, then the interest rate is very important. Ensure your interest rate is competitive with other banks. Consider changing cards to one with a lower interest rate and having the balance of the higher one moved across to the new lower one. Many banks offer low rates to new customers for a 'honeymoon' period. Pay off this balance during this period if you can. Read my book *The Financially Wise Girl's Quick Guide to Eliminating Debt* to get rid of your lingering credit card (and other) debt once and for all, if you need more help with this. Then make sure the card is paid off in full each month.

If you have rewards linked credit cards, be aware of the annual fee. If you are getting less benefit from your rewards than you are getting charged in fees, it might be time to get another card altogether, whether it is a rewards card or not.

Go through your credit card statements carefully and check for any transactions that you can't identify. Credit card theft is rife and could cost you in both money and your credit rating. Check for overseas foreign exchange fee charges on your statement. They could indicate unauthorised transactions.

Be aware too that some retailers charge merchant fees when payments are made with credit card. Most don't, but this is an added cost, so compare that against going to the nearest ATM and possibly incurring fees for a cash withdrawal.

Avoid getting cash advances through your credit card as they usually have very high interest rates which are incurred from the moment the transaction is made, even if you pay your card off every month.

Insurances

When money is tight one year, it can be tempting to let your policy(ies) lapse, especially if you have paid your renewals year after year without ever making a claim.

This may turn out to be a false economy should something happen that requires a claim. Watch any news report or read any media and there will almost always be a story of a car accident or house fire where the owner was uninsured. How do you think this will end for them? How would it end for you if you were in that situation?

Insurance is essential to wealth creation and shouldn't be cancelled to save money in the short term. However, that doesn't mean you shouldn't try and get the best possible deal on your policies. The most important factor to consider is to make sure your policy covers exactly what you want and that you're not paying extra for items you don't need. Also remember that insurance companies rely on you automatically renewing your policy every year without holding them to account. Once again, make them work for your business. Some wholly online insurance providers are able to provide greatly reduced premiums. They don't have expensive overheads, and can pass the savings onto consumers.

When taking out insurance for the first time, be clear about what it is you are insuring and what the value is. For example, if insuring your home and contents consider the replacement cost of rebuilding your house and refurnishing it with the contents. Don't forget items such as window and floor coverings and attached items such as air conditioners, fans and light fittings. Come up with a reasonably accurate replacement cost and call a number of insurers with exactly the same information to get comparative quotes.

Also, do not even consider travelling anywhere, particularly overseas, without travel insurance. Your short, cheap and cheery jaunt can turn into an unbelievably expensive exercise if something happens to you overseas, particularly if you require medical attention. There are far too many stories of people suffering medical emergencies while travelling overseas, who did not have adequate (or even any) travel insurance cover. Even minor things such as lost luggage or delayed flights which cause you to miss connecting flights, can turn into expensive exercises without insurance. There is an old but true travel agent maxim which states that if you can't afford to purchase travel insurance, you can't afford to travel. Be sure to always check the fine print on your travel insurance policy as well.

Take a proactive rather than reactive approach. Doing preventative maintenance on your house, such as checking for termites, checking your roof, taps and water lines for leaks and clearing out your gutters, can obviously save you hefty repair bills and possible insurance claims in the future as well.

The same applies to your motor vehicle. Do you want a fully comprehensive policy or will a third party policy suffice for an older vehicle? Are there discounts applicable for security and theft deterrents? This usually applies to both home and motor vehicle insurances.

You can sometimes make savings on your policy by increasing the applicable excess or deductible. This is the amount you will pay before the insurance company pays the remainder. Usually, the higher this amount, the more savings can be made on an insurance policy.

For medical insurance consider carefully what you actually want from your policy. If you are single with no children, you don't want to take out a fully comprehensive family insurance policy. If you are elderly, you don't need obstetrics cover. Pay only for what you need. When your circumstances change, you can change your policy at that time. Keep records of your medical expenses, as sometimes a tax deduction is possible for expenditure over a certain amount.

Make sure you are aware of all the conditions that accompany your insurance policy. Some home insurance policies require you to phone the insurer if you are going to be away from your home leaving it vacant for a certain period of time; for example, if you will be away on holidays. Some car insurance policies will not allow other people to drive your car, or have restrictions on younger drivers, and of course for a claim to be valid you must always abide by the local driving and vehicle laws.

If you have pets, it could actually be a good idea to look at pet insurance. Like human medicine, pet medicine and care has progressed considerably and animals that were once beyond help can now be saved. Consider your pet's environment and what risks it might encounter and your likely veterinary costs if the worst should happen. Allow for all possibilities such as being hit by vehicles, fights with other animals, bites from snakes, spiders, ticks or eating something that's bad for them.

Consider joining group discount schemes that can negotiate competitive insurance rates due to the buying power of a large group.

White Goods, Electrical and Furniture

Never pay full price for any new electrical goods or furniture if you can avoid it. The listed price is usually open for negotiation. Learn the art of bargaining. Don't be afraid to ask for a discount or better pricing. If you don't ask, the answer is already no. Be prepared to walk away unless your price is met, unless the item is an absolute bargain already.

When looking for new appliances, make sure you check out their power consumption efficiency. Newer appliances are required to meet stricter guidelines for power and water usage. Sometimes a more expensive item with better power consumption can actually save you more money in the longer term.

If your refrigerator is still working well, but your power consumption is high, have the seals looked at and replaced if necessary. These lose effectiveness over time and don't seal as well, letting out the cool air and possibly putting your food at risk from bacterial contamination. Also make sure you defrost the freezer component regularly if it is not a frost-free model. These simple tips can be cheaper than buying a replacement item and can also save a significant amount of your electricity costs.

With second-hand items, it is always a case of buyer beware, but quite often there is a perfectly legitimate reason the item is being sold.

Some areas to consider:

- **Auctions.** Many auction places act as clearing houses for local furniture and electrical supply stores. Always take advantage of the inspections prior to the auction. In most cases, if you are the successful bidder, you have to take the item as is, although in many cases for brand new items, there is a limited warranty from the auction house.
- **Sales.** After Christmas, mid-year or other sales periods are great times to replace an old and worn item with a new one.
- **Floor stock.** Ask whether the floor display stock can be purchased at a discounted price.
- **Factory seconds/scratch and dent sales.** These products have generally not met specific criteria for sale at full retail price, but still function normally. They may contain superficial or cosmetic defects or damage such as scratches or dents which will not detract from their performance, or it could be as simple as the item not

having any packaging. They usually still have full manufacturer's warranty, however, always check first.
- **Buy out of season.** Purchase big ticket items such as air conditioners and swimming pools in winter and heaters in summer or when on sale after winter.
- **Second-hand.** You don't have to purchase new items, particularly if you're renting or just starting out. Second-hand and charity stores often have a range of electrical and furniture items that are perfectly acceptable and may even have been refurbished.
- **Pawn shops.** Many have an extensive range of household items.
- **Classifieds.** Scour your local newspaper advertisements and check your local online private sales sites.
- **People moving.** People are more mobile these days. However they don't always take everything with them and don't want to throw away perfectly good, working and serviceable items or cart them to the local charity shop when moving or relocating. Blended families often have to sell or get rid of their duplicate items when they move into one residence and older retiring couples often have a large household of items that they need to significantly reduce when they move into smaller and more manageable accommodation.
- If buying new from a larger traditional retailer (at a discount of course), take advantage of interest free periods, if available. However, ensure you make all the necessary payments before the interest charges apply. They can be extremely high and, more often than not, apply to the whole amount from the time you made the purchase, not from the date the interest charges start or on the outstanding amount. As with anything, read the fine print and make sure you know all the conditions.

Jillian's old computer was on its last legs and she decided to look for another one. After doing her research she found a brand that was reliable and would run her required software satisfactorily. She shopped around and found the model she was after at a large electrical chain store, who offered her a repayment plan. It could be repaid over three years with an interest free period of one year. As she had time to repay it, rather than pay it all upfront, she decided to add a printer to her purchase and signed up for the repayment deal.

After researching the deal, she worked out that after the interest free period her repayments would rise dramatically and would incur a 20% interest charge on the total amount. Furthermore, if she made just the minimum payments over the three year period, she would have paid nearly twice the initial purchase price by which time the computer would be almost obsolete. She calculated how much her repayments would be if she broke it down into the one year interest free period, and then rather than paying if off monthly, she made fortnightly payments, as that was the same as her pay cycle.

Not only did she pay it off before the one year interest free period ended, she had also proactively approached her bank to see if she could take out a loan if required, should a balance remain after the 12 months, to take advantage of the much lower interest rate offered by the bank.

Utilities (Electricity, Phones, Cable, Water and Gas)

With all your utility providers, make sure you audit them at least once a year to see if they are still giving you the best value for money.

"Shadow shop" or call your existing providers as a potential new customer to see if they are offering new and better deals than the one you currently have.

As per the insurance post, consider joining group discount schemes that negotiate great deals for their members.

Electricity

Some areas to look at:

- Turn off appliances at the wall when you're not using them. Most modern appliances, especially ones with remote controls, operate in a 'standby' mode, so they can be activated as soon as they receive a signal from the remote or when switched on. To do this they draw small amounts of power continually. However, this continual power usage adds to the bottom line of your electricity bill.
- Change your lights to more energy efficient bulbs. Turn them off when not in the room.
- Insulation in your roof and walls can save on heating and cooling costs.
- Only boil as much water as you need instead of filling the kettle to maximum.

- If you are able to, take advantage of the sun and hang your washing up outside rather than use a dryer.
- When charging your mobile or cell phone, tablet or MP3 player, try to charge them during the day rather than overnight, as they usually only charge in about three or four hours. It is also possible to overcharge some of the older batteries, which may cause them to swell.
- Do all your ironing in one go. Heating an iron a number of times to do just one or two items uses more electricity than doing all your ironing at once. Start with the lowest heat settings and work up to the highest ones. Turn it off when you are ironing your last item. The residual heat in the iron will be sufficient to complete the garment.
- Make sure things like pool pumps and hot water services are on a cheaper tariff.
- Have your air conditioner serviced once a year, or at least make sure you clean out the filters and ducts. These tend to collect dust over the course of the year, which lowers their efficiency and can add considerably to your power costs when cooling or heating.
- If you own your own home, investigate a solar energy system, either for hot water, electricity or both.
- If renting you could favour potential rental properties that have solar electricity, hot water or both, as this will significantly cut down on your expenses, as will gas hot water and cooking appliances.

Telephones and Communications

Make sure you regularly check your particular phone and data plan to see if it still suits you.

- Check your data usage and see if are using your entire designated quota.

- If you are constantly going over your quota, call your carrier to see if you can get a better deal.
- Change to a lower plan if required.
- If you are always below your data quota you could use some of your data for Skype phone calls. This will save you on telephone costs and will use up the excess monthly data, which might ordinarily go to waste.
- Look at other carriers. Call them and see what their rates are, and whether they're comparable to your current plan. Play them off against each other. They all want your business.
- Are you getting all the benefits you are entitled to under your cable plan? If not, and if you're unlikely to make full use of all the features you're paying for but not really using, then downgrade your subscription.

Water

Some areas to look at:

- Change your shower head to a water efficient model.
- Use the washing machine or dishwasher only once you have a full load.
- While on these appliances, check the water efficiency rating when looking for a new washing machine or dishwasher. A more expensive but better water and energy efficient model will save you money in the long term.
- Are you able to reuse or recycle the rinse water from your washing machine or dishwasher? Check if you can recirculate water for the garden or for flushing toilets.
- Consider installing a dual flush toilet system.
- If you have a water meter and can access it, check your usage occasionally. To do this, ensure all taps are turned off and not being used, then check the figure on the meter. Wait an hour without using any water and

check the meter again. If the number has increased, there may be a leak in the water pipes somewhere. Paying a plumber to fix this now could save considerable money over time. Have them repair or replace leaky taps and toilets at the same time.
- Consider installing a water tank to collect rainwater that can be plumbed to your toilets, or can be used for the garden or washing the car.

Saving on Your Health

Your health is your wealth. And this is meant in a literal sense. When you are well, you're not using money for doctor's visits, medication, other practitioners and time off work for recovery. Make 'prevention rather than cure' your mantra, as prevention is not only better, it's also cheaper than the cure.

The 'secret' of good health is not really a secret at all. Just:

- Ensure you have at least five servings of different vegetables and two pieces of different fruit every day;
- Have a handful of mixed nuts and seeds;
- Don't overeat, or at least don't take in more energy than you expend out;
- Consider a good quality (preferably organic) vitamin and mineral supplement;
- Eliminate or limit consumption of processed food;
- Have a bit of everything but in moderation;
- Get daily exercise;
- Try to be out in the sunshine for 20 minutes either in the early morning or late afternoon.

Check with your doctor about what free screening programs exist and take advantage of these, e.g., mammogram services, bowel cancer screening. Some pharmacies can carry out free blood pressure checks.

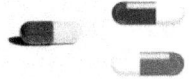

If you do require medicines, however, you may want to consider buying generic brands. Generic medications are copies of popular branded medications once the patent has expired and they are legally required to have the same active ingredients. They are usually (though not always) identical to their branded counterparts. In fact some are even made by the same company, but are considerably cheaper. Make use of discount pharmacy chains and warehouses, which are usually much cheaper than other pharmacies.

Reduce your alcohol intake. The recommended weekly alcohol intake is just that: a recommendation. It's not a target to be reached. While it's nice to share a glass with good friends and food, drinking too much is neither good for your health nor your wallet. Try to calculate this in terms of opportunity cost. How much do you spend on alcohol in a week, a month, a year? And to what better purpose could you use those funds?

While we're on the topic of drinks, cut down on soft drinks, sodas and pop too. These are basically carbonated water with added refined white sugar or worse – artificial sweeteners, artificial colours and flavours and increasingly, caffeine. There is nothing redeeming about soft drinks. They contain no nutrients whatsoever and are highly acidic, which is extremely bad for our bodies (in a healthy state our bodies are alkaline) and for our teeth. Drink water.

Cut down on meat. People from developing countries are increasing their meat consumption and they have a corresponding rise in the types of diseases associated with most developed countries. The healthiest cultures in the world do eat meat, but very sparingly, not half a cow at a time. They also consume many fresh fruits, berries, vegetables, beans and legumes, nuts, whole grains and seeds, cold pressed virgin oils, butters and cold water fish. There are a few other factors, such as living much more simply and connecting with family, friends and nature, but their diets of mainly unprocessed food and minimal meat can mean better health and potential longevity. I'm not advocating becoming a full vegetarian or vegan, unless that's what you practice already. Enjoy a steak or roast chicken if that's what you like. But in moderation and have some meat free days during the week.

Cut out or cut down on junk food and takeaways. It may seem like a quick fix to overcome an immediate hunger, but some planning ahead should alleviate or greatly reduce this with the meal planning tips listed previously.

Fast food should be a very occasional, with emphasis again on the *very occasional,* treat. It's not one of your daily food groups.

Eating fast food begins a terrible cycle that can be hard to escape from. There is very little nutritional value in fast food. Because of this, your body doesn't receive its required quota of nutrients, vitamins and minerals after you've eaten it, and your hypothalamus or appestat tells you to eat again. You're hungry earlier than if you had eaten a more nutrient dense food. So you get into a vicious circle of eating more and more junk food, but not getting the nutrients you require. Your body needs to be nourished, not just fed. Snack on nuts and homemade popcorn instead. Eat more whole foods and your body will get the nutrients it requires, and you won't waste money on junk food.

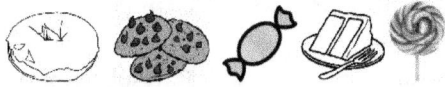

Included in the junk food category are things like sweets, lollies, candy, cakes, biscuits, cookies, doughnuts and chocolate, basically anything that contains highly refined flours and sugars and hydrogenated fats. Make no mistake, none of these things are compatible with a healthy human body. Save your money and don't buy these things, or only have them as a *very occasional* treat. These things should not be part of your daily menu.

Quit smoking. This really is a no brainer. Honestly, who doesn't know in this day and age the negative consequences of smoking? Not just for yourself, your health and your looks but also for the people around you, especially young children and pets.

Obviously the best way to stop smoking is to never start in the first place. However, it may not be that simple if you are already a smoker. Please, do your health, skin and your hip pocket a favour and do whatever it takes to give up smoking.

If you need an incentive (really, what more incentive do you need than to know that you will most likely NOT die a horrible and painful death AND look at least 20 years older), work out how much this habit is costing you every year. Then think of it purely in self-indulgent terms, not even in terms of savings, looks or your health. It's just an opportunity cost exercise. Could this be a relaxing holiday by the beach or hotel pool? A ski holiday? An adventure holiday? Could this be the latest entertainment system? Could this be a whole new summer or winter wardrobe? A whole cupboard of shoes or jewellery? Or even a new car? Think about it.

Look after your teeth. Getting into the habit of regular flossing and brushing your teeth can save you an enormous amount in dental bills later.

Subscriptions/Memberships

Do you have any memberships and subscriptions that you pay annually but don't actually use that you could cancel? These could include things like:

- Gym memberships;
- Magazines, periodicals, newspapers, web sites;
- Sporting clubs;
- Airline or travel clubs;
- Entertainment memberships;
- Professional bodies;
- Monthly access fees; for example, trading information;
- Software;
- Donations.

If you're not using it, it's just wasting your money. However you don't want to cancel every one of your memberships or subscriptions, just the ones you don't need or use. Some, like auto club membership, you do actually want to keep for safety and peace of mind, even if you haven't used them for a while. And of course, if you are actually going to the gym keep your membership.

Make sure you check your credit card for automatic renewals for memberships and subscriptions that you might have forgotten about but for which you are still getting charged.

Travelling

There are many savings that can be made when travelling. Use deal sites (see below) to get good pricing on airfares, hotels and holidays.

Travel during shoulder or off peak times if possible, where you can still take advantage of the climate or conditions, but it's just on either side of the peak season. You can still have a great ski holiday or beach holiday or travel to the Greek Isles just before or after the peak times, and still take advantage of the snow or sun and tourist attractions. School holidays also tend to drive up prices of flights and accommodation, but the weeks just before or after are substantially cheaper. As well as saving on the costs, you also have the added benefit of fewer tourists in the area you're visiting and shorter queues at the attractions.

This can be more difficult if you work in the education system or have school-aged children, but could you take the first or last week of a school term or semester off for a holiday? Can you work an educational angle into the holiday?

Subscribe to airline, resort and hotel mailing lists so you can be informed when sales and cheaper prices are available. Travel agents always have discounted fares and holiday package deals in their windows. Airfares for very early morning or late evening flights are usually cheaper than peak during the day fares.

Consider AirBnB and couch surfing type websites. They can be much cheaper than hotel accommodation with the added advantage of having local knowledge on tap.

Deal and Group Buying Discount Sites

There are now a great number of deal sites available worldwide. These are sites like Scoopon and Groupon, which exist almost globally, but there are certainly other deal sites operating in other countries. Some of these sites target specific industries, such as travel, hotels or clothing, and others are generic, offering all types of products and services with daily deals.

This can be a great way of obtaining items or services at heavily discounted prices, but make sure you read the fine print. Some deals can only be redeemed on specific days, date ranges or times and may not suit you at all. There can be myriad conditions attached, so be warned. However, if you find something that you're after at a discounted price, absolutely take advantage of it.

Deal sites can be a great way of purchasing gifts which are slightly more personalised than just a generic gift card. When you are trying to save money, special days such as Christmas, birthdays, anniversaries, Mother's and Father's days can be a big drain on your savings plan. Start looking at obtaining these gifts well in advance and take advantage of sales.

Take advantage of coupon books, which offers discounts on meals, flights, hotel accommodation, car rental and many other everyday items.

Some supermarket chains print offers on the back of their receipts or dockets offering discounts on countless products and services from restaurant meals to carpet cleaning.

Babies and Children

Children can absolutely gobble through your money like there's no tomorrow, but you can still make considerable savings with regard to babies and children's items.

Babies, especially in their first few years, grow at phenomenal rates. They only wear their clothes for a short period of time before they've outgrown them, particularly when seasons change from summer to winter and back. Second-hand babies and children's clothing is a great avenue for making savings. If you are in a playgroup or mother's group, share your clothes amongst each other. Check out your local classifieds, eBay and other local sales websites for people selling their baby clothes. Investigate clothing "swap" groups where you can swap your baby clothes for others in different sizes.

If your friends and siblings have children that are older than yours, you can buy their baby furniture from them. Cots, change tables, baby baths, high chairs for feeding, car capsules and booster seats have to be made to a specific standard and are usually very sturdy and robust to withstand the rough and tumble of daily life with babies and small children. Many toys can also be passed onto new families, particularly if they're constructed from easy to clean and disinfect materials, such as plastic.

You will also be given many new items from friends and family. Once your children have outgrown these items, you can in turn pass them on or on-sell them through eBay and your local selling sites.

Check out bulk buying for things like nappies. Team up with other mothers requiring the same items. Usually with these bulk buys, the more you buy, the cheaper the unit cost of each item.

Learn or rediscover the lost arts of sewing, knitting and crocheting. Each item will be unique, and these make great gifts too.

Check out factory clearance houses and also auctions. These places often sell boxes of new clothing that haven't sold for whatever reason, with tags still attached from department and retail stores. There are usually varying sizes in the box, so keep larger sizes for when your child is older or sell or pass on any items you don't want.

Entertainment

Saving money doesn't mean you have to sit at home all the time and not go out and have fun. There are ways of saving money on treats and having fun without breaking the bank.

Everyone loves going to the movies. It's nice to take a break and have some time out, but a day or night out at the movies can be an expensive exercise once you have to factor in parking, meals, snacks as well as the movie tickets for everyone. But it doesn't have to be hugely expensive. Firstly, become familiar with all your local cinemas, and know their ticket prices, which can vary greatly.

Deciding which cinema you go to depends on whether you are going with children (as many of the cheaper ones are usually more child friendly) or having a girl's night out with friends (in which case you probably want to go a little more upmarket). You can still save though. The candy bars associated with cinemas have huge profit margins and large mark ups on their products. Think about bringing your own snacks to minimise or eliminate the need to buy food or drinks at the venue. Bring your own water bottle and something healthy, such as nuts or rice or corn crackers. Bring a banana and some cherries or pre-cut up fruit such as apples and oranges.

If you are a regular cinema goer, consider becoming a member of the cinema chain, if they have memberships, as this usually entitles you to cheaper tickets. Buy your tickets in bulk, say in lots of five or ten tickets, as these are usually discounted. These can also make great gifts. Consider waiting and buying a movie on DVD. You'll be able to watch it over and over whenever you want, along with your friends, and this is especially useful if you have children.

Visit your local art galleries and museums. Most of them are free or have minimal entry costs and are a great way of increasing your knowledge and spending a lovely afternoon soaking up the local culture.

Many of the larger galleries will have special events, such as exhibitions by particular artists where you can see their best works, usually on loan from other galleries around the world, for a period of time.

If your treat is going to the theatre, investigate your local amateur theatres and check out their programs. Many of these are springboards for aspiring actors who start out in community and small theatre companies. You can see many of the classics performed by amateurs and it is an opportunity to see up-and-coming actors before they become well known.

Many professional productions at the bigger theatres offer tickets to the full dress rehearsals before the debut performance. This is a great way of seeing the big names and their performance before the first run in your city. Quite often the large professional ballet and opera productions can also be seen this way. Check with your local theatre's box office to see if you can obtain tickets for these. Once again, buying in bulk might give you cheaper pricing, so check with your friends for interest in upcoming performances.

Eating out as a treat doesn't have to break the bank. There are savings that can be made by using coupons that allow group discounts as a percentage of the total cost or a free main course for every purchased main course. Check out the daily specials available on deal sites (see above). Some restaurants have a cheaper menu for their slow days or nights to try and fill up tables, so consider booking your night out for dinner on a day other than the more popular Friday nights or weekends. As listed above on the deal sites section, check out your coupon books and the back of your shopping receipts for deals. You can most likely have a great meal at a great price and discover a new restaurant at the same time.

"Wow," said Daria nodding, "there are so many areas where I can find savings. I just haven't seen them."

Sage agreed. "And those were just a few examples. I'm sure you'll find many more – once you start looking, you'll find them everywhere. Remember, the price is usually negotiable. If you don't ask, the answer is already no."

Daria leaned back in her chair and sighed with satisfaction. She had learned a lot over the past few weeks.

She looked over at her friend. "Sage, thank you so much for your help. I can take responsibility for my savings now, and I'm going to have fun finding bargains and new ways to save money."

Sage smiled at her friend. "Good luck. I know you can do it."

FINANCIALLY WISE ACTION PLAN –

Start implementing some of the ways of saving money listed here, and then come up with more ideas of your own.

Make sure you put the money you have saved to good use by putting it into your savings, investing it or reducing debt.

Notes:

_____

_____

_____

_____

_____

9 TEN MONTHS LATER

"Wow, it's a beauty!" Sage exclaimed, as she examined Daria's new car.

"Oh, it's so good. It starts every time, even in cold weather, never breaks down and the ride is so smooth. It has all the mod cons and, best of all, the mechanic has all the parts," Daria enthused.

"I put as much as I could into my car savings account until I had the full amount. I also followed your suggestions on what to do when researching and buying a car. I was able to negotiate the price down with the dealer because I was paying cash," she continued.

Sage smiled at Daria over the roof of the car. "You bought really well." She opened the driver's door and poked her head inside and then straightened up again and looked at Daria in surprise.

"It still has the new car smell inside, I thought this was a second-hand car," she said.

"Oh, it is, it's a year old. I didn't want to buy a new car as it would have lost its value too quickly after I'd bought it," Daria confirmed.

She smiled at Sage, "I've been continuing with my financial education and that was another thing I learned."

Sage nodded in approval. "That's great to hear, I'm really impressed," she said.

Daria's smile turned into a grin. "Here's another thing I picked up, and I'm more than happy to share this knowledge with you."

She reached into her handbag, pulled out a small spray bottle and said, "It's a car air freshener. The scent is called 'New Car Smell', " and they both burst into laughter.

10 END NOTE

Hello, it's Kathy again. I hope you found this book useful, and it provided you with some money saving tips. I hope you have also been inspired to set up a system for implementing your very own personal savings plan.

Once you are confident with your savings regime, you might like to check out my other finance starter books to help you:

- Before You Buy That! The Financially Wi$e Girl's Quick Guide to Budgeting
- Oops Overdrawn! The Financially Wi$e Girl's Quick Guide to Eliminating Debt
- Turn Those Taps On! The Financially Wi$e Girl's Quick Guide to Creating Multiple Streams of Income; and
- Finally Free! The Financially Wi$e Girl's Quick Guide to Calculating Retirement Income.

If this book has helped you, please let me know and tell your friends.

Visit www.financiallywise.com.au and tell everyone how you are going with your savings plan and download your free reports.

RESOURCES

Books

All the books in the Financially Wise beginners series
The Richest Man in Babylon, George S Clason
Think and Grow Rich, Napoleon Hill
Rich Dad Poor Dad, Robert Kiyosaki
Rich Woman, Kim Kiyosaki
The Millionaire Next Door, Thomas J. Stanley & William D. Danko
The Woman's Money Book, Vivienne James
You Were Born Rich, Bob Proctor
A Man is not a Financial Plan, Joan Baker
Who Moved My Cheese?, Dr Spencer Johnson
The One Minute Millionaire, Mark Victor Hanson & Robert G. Allen
The Savvy Girl's Money Book, Emily Chantiri
The Magic of Thinking Big, David J Schwartz
Put More Cash in Your Pocket, Loral Langemeier
Secrets of the Millionaire Mind, T. Harv Eker
Nice Girls Don't Get Rich, Lois P. Frankel
The Angel Inside, Chris Widener
Wink and Grow Rich, Roger Hamilton
The Automatic Millionaire and *Smart Women Finish Rich*, David Bach
What I Didn't Learn at School But Wish I Had, Jamie McIntyre
All the books in the Rich Dad Poor Dad series
Any book by or about Richard Branson
Any book by Anthony Robbins
Any book by Dr John DeMartini
Any book by Jim Rohn
Any book by Brian Tracy
Any book by Denis Waitley
Any book by Pat Mesiti

Websites

Check out your bank's website. Most of them have a "saving calculator" or just Google "saving calculator" and it will bring up your local banks and other local websites.

www.financiallywise.com.au

www.richwoman.com

www.richdad.com

www.simplesavings.com.au

www.jimrohn.com

www.briantracy.com

www.zerohedge.com

www.usdebtclock.org

www.australiandebtclock.com.au

www.nationaldebtclocks.org - select your country from list or add /debtclock/[your country] to the URL, eg:
www.nationaldebtclocks.org/debtclock/unitedkingdom

THE OTHER FINANCIALLY WISE BOOKS IN THIS BEGINNERS SERIES

Before You Buy That! The Financially Wi$e Girl's Quick Guide to Budgeting.

Daria has an "unexpected" large bill due shortly that she needs to pay. When Wise Owl questions her more closely, it turns out it wasn't really unexpected, she was just hoping it was going to show up a bit later than it did.

Join Daria as Wise Owl helps her to set up her budget. She finds out it's not as bad or as boring as she thought, and she is now much more in control of her finances. Now that she has set up her budget, she can quickly work out what her expenditure is likely to be from month to month and beyond.

This makes planning a breeze and she knows what her expenses are likely to be for the whole year.

And you can enjoy the same freedom from worrying about the future and where your money is going by setting up your own budget. Once it's done it's easy to keep to and update.

Oops, Overdrawn! The Financially Wi$e Girl's Quick Guide to Eliminating Debt.

Daria's sister is in trouble with all her credit card debt. She's borrowing from one card to pay off another, and that doesn't even take into account her other debts, such as a car loan and store cards.

Daria can't help her as she has a few debts of her own.

Wise Owl helps Daria (and various members of Daria's family) go through all their debts and work out plans to pay them all off over a period of time and then completely eliminate them. Then they can remain debt free forever.

Once you know their formula, you too can pay off all your debts and eliminate debt repayments forever!

Turn Those Taps On! The Financially Wi$e Girl's Quick Guide to Creating Multiple Streams of Income.

Daria's cousin loses her job and she doesn't know what to do. She's having trouble finding another one and she's not sure if she should return to school to add to her skills so she might be able to find a job in another field.

Daria wants to help her cousin and turns to Wise Own for advice.

Wise Owl explains to Daria and her cousin (and other friends) why exchanging your time for money in a traditional job is the worst way of earning money. Wise Owl then goes on to describe ways of creating multiple streams of active and passive income that she, her family and friends could consider. A job is but one stream.

There are a few streams you could consider adding to your income as well. Not all of them will suit everyone, but everyone should consider having more than just one stream of income.

Finally Free! The Financially Wi$e Girl's Quick Guide to Calculating Retirement Income.

Daria's parents are considering retirement. It should be an exciting time. But they're worried. They don't think they have enough money to retire comfortably and they don't have a lot of time left to try and boost their retirement income.

They ask Daria for advice and Daria asks her friend and mentor Wise Owl for help.

Wise Owl shows Daria and her family how to calculate how much money each of them might need to have to retire comfortably.

Daria goes through the calculations to work out her retirement figure and her parents go through various scenarios and options to help see them through their retirement.

You too should be looking at how much you would like or need at retirement. The sooner you start, the more you'll have.

ABOUT THE AUTHOR

Kathy Ran lives in Brisbane, Australia, with her two children and cat. She continues her financial education every day with extensive reading lists and regular attendance of educational seminars, while also running a number of businesses.

She is a very firm believer in financial education for everyone and her purpose is to financially educate everyone around the world. She provides financial coaching services and is in the process of developing courses, applications and educational programs to spread the financial education message.

If you think you could benefit from some financial coaching or you'd like further information and learn some more, please visit Kathy's website – www.financiallywise.com.au, send a message through the Contact Us page and while you're there check out the articles and reports.

Feel free to drop her a line through the website or through any of the sources below if you think she might be able to help you with something, leave a comment or share your story. Make sure you check back regularly as the information is always being updated and new articles added.

Connect with Kathy at:

www.facebook.com/financiallywise
https://twitter.com/financiallywis1
https://au.linkedin.com/pub/kathy-ran
https://plus.google.com/+FinanciallywiseAuFinanciallyWise
www.youtube.com/c/FinanciallywiseAuFinanciallyWise
www.slideshare.net/financiallywise

www.ingramcontent.com/pod-product-compliance
Lightning Source LLC
Chambersburg PA
CBHW051728170526
45167CB00002B/841